Face to Face with God

Healing the Cry Within

Deb Copeland
Janice Davis

Two Women's Conversations of Unending Love ~ Amazing Grace

Xulon
PRESS

And be not conformed to this world: but be ye transformed by the renewing of your mind, that ye may prove what [is] that good, and acceptable, and perfect, will of God. (Romans 12:2)

Dedication

This book is dedicated to the multitudes of men and women who believe no one understands what they're going through, who have lost all hope of a more meaningful life, and through no fault of their own are suffering from past hurts and rejections, and have grown weary of trusting anyone. Our greatest hope is for you to see the *Pearl of Great Price* you are and how deeply you are loved by the Father. Be of good courage, your life is about to change. Our prayer is that each of you will embrace the truths penned in this book, and will apply them to your lives with the expectation of a more abundant life, full of joy and peace. Let your heart and mind be renewed.

Deb's Acknowledgements

*F*irst I would like to thank God for redeeming me, and for carrying me in the palm of His nail scared hand. A special thanks to my husband, my children, and my grandchildren who have taught me what family is all about.

I am truly indebted to my husband, Don Lucci, for his constant love, prayers, and support. I am especially thankful for his heart for God.

A special recognition to all of my prayer partners who stood in the gap constantly praying that God would lead and direct my steps according to His will for my life and the penning of this book. Without your support this book wouldn't have been written. I am most appreciative of my new best friend Dr. Lynette Weist, without your awesome Christian guidance, I would be in a very dark place. A special thank you to all of the friends and relatives who took time daily from their hectic lives to confirm my story and the life I lived. Without your honesty I would still be lost and afraid.

Janice's Acknowledgements

I want to thank my husband, Gene Davis, who has challenged me to grow up spiritually into the things of God; to my boys, Stephen, Preston, Brooks and Clay, who have supported me with their undying love; and to the Scroll Scribes writers' group I attended, for their continued support and encouragement. I couldn't have done it without your unwavering faith that God was speaking, and had chosen an unlikely vessel to bring forth words of healing to the emotionally wounded. Many thanks to my pastor, Bishop Hugh Arnold, and the members of Ivory Palace Church International, who always make me feel loved and accepted. Most of all I want to thank my Heavenly Father for His love, grace, mercy, and for trusting me to speak His words of truth to the world.

Table of Contents

Introduction

Attitude Begins with Us

Deb: *Face 2 Face with God: Healing the Cry Within* had to be written. Why? Because it has been in the making for over fifty-six years, but it wasn't until I met Janice Davis, whom I will introduce you to very soon, that I had the courage to do so. For many years, I was barely surviving emotionally, although on the outside I appeared to have it altogether. I carried a lot of emotional baggage which revealed itself through fear, resentment, anger, isolation, rejection, shame, heartache, and confusion. I was emotionally abandoned as a toddler, suffered physical, mental, and sexual abuse as a young child, and was rejected by my father as an adolescent. In later years, I became a successful entrepreneur, burying myself in my work. I was a life coach helping others, and an acclaimed motivational speaker traveling across the United States bringing messages of hope and empowerment, and teaching others about the role "attitude" plays in our lives. I went on to author a couple of books, one of which was, *Attitude Therapy,* published in 2006.

Although I was providing hope to others in the work place daily, I still continued to feel restless. I kept hearing a whisper calling me to help others in a far more profound and meaningful way. The voice I heard calling me was the voice of my **best** friend, God saying, "If you can travel speaking to audiences as an entrepreneur, making money for the National Consulting Group I gave you, how much more could you be doing for Me?" Having successfully authored two books, owned multiple businesses, and enjoyed much praise and honor so early in my life, certainly I could draw a crowd to do this for our Lord and Savior. I can tell you I'm happier working for Christ than I've ever been. Then He presented me with what would prove to be my single most difficult task, which included working with another of His children. Read on.

I was sitting in a little restaurant on Hilton Head Island, SC, one Sunday with my family, when a lady approached our table.

Genuinely and quietly she spoke to me and said, "I couldn't help but overhear your love for Jesus Christ, and I have to say that we both share in that love and adoration of our Lord and Savior."

I immediately stood up and not only did our eyes and hands connect, so did our souls. It was like running into a childhood friend; we embraced and shared our common interest and love for God. May I introduce you to Janice Davis?

Janice: The day we met truly was an answer to prayer. I had been working in the restaurant since the first part of the summer, and knew my time there would be short. I even mentioned to my husband that God had me working there for a reason. As the tourist season drew to a close, I still didn't know why I was there. On that fateful Sunday little did I know the direction of my life was about to change. I have to admit I did contemplate whether or not I should come over to your table. I didn't want to seem forward, but I just had to share with you my love for our Lord and Savior Jesus Christ. It was clearly evident to me that you had a genuine relationship with Him, and when I saw your love for Him I just had to speak up. It was so refreshing to hear someone else speaking about His presence in their lives. Now here we are some four months later writing together. I have learned over the years to never underestimate God's ability to change our lives, or His awesome power to change our well thought out plans. I know the Holy Spirit brought us together for a purpose and that is to help one another and to inspire others.

Deb: What a "God thing" that He introduced us to each other that day. He brought two wounded souls together just one week after I completely surrendered the deepest darkest secrets of my soul, and prayed for Him to heal me spiritually, physically, mentally, and emotionally. For the first time in my life, I had finally opened up and told Him the secrets of my childhood shame.

Janice: Isn't that just like God? He recognizes our need for help and sends someone into our lives who understands us and doesn't sit in the seat of judgment. Honestly, I had never met another person who I thought was like me in the oddest sense. So when you and I first met I thought to myself, "Thank you Lord for sending me a friend who is just as weird as I am in that she loves you with all she has." When I say "weird," I mean it in a good way. God's Word says it so beautifully about Godly friendships. "[As] iron sharpens iron, so a man sharpens the countenance of his friend" (Proverbs 27:17). Deb, not only have you been an encouragement to my life, you have also helped to sharpen me spiritually in deepening my desire to serve Him all the more.

If we will let Him, God can take all our pain and suffering to glorify Himself. Deb, you and I both know what suffering is all about. The many years of wrestling with our own emotional pain has taught us complete dependence on God. You see, in God nothing is ever wasted. You and I both have been through our own share of troubles, and many times it has seemed as if the problems we faced were insurmountable. But through it all we discovered real hope when we called out to our loving Heavenly Father.

Our vision for this book is to give each of you the hope and confidence needed to build a joyous future for yourself and your family. The road to healing is never easy, and will surely be paved with personal challenges to both encourage and build you spiritually from the inside out. Not only will you grow, you will also develop a desire to become the person our Creator intended you to be. A relationship with Jesus Christ is the only answer to a broken life.

Deb, He is the reason you and I have overcome the odds, and He wants us to share with others how they, too, can experience the same kind of freedom we have found. Our relationship with Him has brought us tremendous joy and a quiet peace amidst the troubled waters of our lives so circumstances no longer dictate how we think or feel. When trouble does come, as it surely will, you and I will both rest in the knowledge that "all is well with our souls." Deb, as we think back to those early days when our lives were unbearable and full of pain, we are overjoyed in the newfound freedom we have discovered. Our invitation to others is, "Come! Let us share with you how you, too, can be **free!**"

Deb: Janice, you have not only inspired me, but you have also motivated me to step out of my comfort zone. I, too, feel your love for Him. I can't wait to see what God will do with our relationship and how He will use us together.

Chapter 1

Why a Godly Attitude Counts

Not only so, but we also glory in our sufferings, because we know that suffering produces perseverance, perseverance, character and character, hope. And hope does not put us to shame, because God's love has been poured out into our hearts through the Holy Spirit, who has been given to us. (Romans 5:3-5 NIV)

Deb: "Attitude is not about what happens to us in life but rather how we respond"[1] was both the purpose and tag line of my first book *Attitude Therapy*, published in 2006. As I continue to interview and mentor, I still strongly believe it to be as true today as it was back then when I wrote the book. People have it down right tough, and their very existence brings them pain and suffering, often through no fault of their own. Just this week I interviewed a beautiful woman, whose beauty was obvious both inside and out. My heart broke as I listened attentively to the graphic and horrific details of her abuse. I felt like I was suffering with her. The next day, my mind kept drifting back to her story as I thought about what she had shared with me. It was not like I suffered her painful agony, torment and torture, but rather I felt her pain as she struggles through life.

The pain and suffering I am talking about affects our work, relationships with others, and every fiber of our being. It complicates the issues we are working through as well as any glimpses of hope and happiness along the way. **Attitude** isn't always training our minds to the psychologies of whether we choose to see the glass half-empty or half-full, nor is it about taking away from church only those things which are healthy and good. Please understand me; I am speaking of moving to another level of *Attitude Therapy*, *God-a-tude therapy*, if you will. What I mean is learning to have a brand new attitude in Christ Jesus by allowing our sufferings to produce perseverance, character, and hope. Our attitudes belong to us. Our attitude is in our DNA! Simply put, an attitude comes from thoughts and feelings evoked by a person or event that leads to an ongoing habitual mindset producing the same response [feelings+thoughts+behavior] over and over again. Until we place our attitude at His feet we will continue to produce the same results through habitual behavior. Philippians 2:5 states; "In your relationships with one another, have the same mindset as Christ Jesus" NIV

Janice: What is a godly attitude anyway, and why is it so important to our outlook on life? I will surmise that most of us probably have never contemplated what it means to have a good attitude, much less a godly one, but rest assured it matters every day.

Deb: I hear you loud and clear. As I have taught and preached on *Attitude Therapy* for twenty-five years, "Attitude isn't what happens to us in life, but rather how we respond." But I must say God has placed on my heart something bigger to pursue and that is Christian attitudes. It is my belief that as Christians we should be held more accountable for our "stinkin' thinkin'."

I am going to confess to you something I haven't told anyone until now. I am the writer and author of *Attitude Therapy,* the expert from afar, the teacher, the mentor, the acclaimed motivational speaker, and the attitude guru who still has trouble with her attitude unless I converse with God.

Janice: As a teenager and on into my twenties, I wasn't aware just how much attitude mattered. I have found it matters to your spouse, your family, and your friends, as well as your colleagues. In fact it has an effect on everyone and anyone who is a constant in your life; even those who randomly come in and out. It says a lot about the kind of person we are, whether we anticipate the outcome of life to be good, or our expectations are full of gloom and despair. Back during my college days, I lived with a family of seven children. I vividly remember their mother teaching them the importance of having a "good attitude." I didn't quite get what it was all about until I started having children of my own, and then I understood what she meant. Attitude can make or break our relationships with others and even with ourselves. That's how important it is for us to develop right attitudes. And I do say develop because carnally we have the capability to change ourselves from the inside out just by the way we think and behave, but with God's help we can develop godly attitudes.

Deb: Negative thinking is a disease that should require a twelve-step program as well as deprogramming clinics for those who want freedom. I believe negative self-talk tears down marriages, families and lives, not to mention a person's self-worth. Negative speaking is so destructive to both the author of the words and the victim of their malice. Negativity not only destroys peace, hope, and joy, but it interferes with our ability to receive God's grace and love. How can we receive the intended meaning of a message if it is blocked with deep-seated negative feelings?

I believe negativity is the number one tool in Satan's arsenal. As you know, I mentor a lot of women and youth, and I share with them our need for spiritually positive tools to be in place before we come under attack. That means prior to leaving our beds in the morning we should be prayed up with God's words of life so that we are able to repel the negative words of others. I teach my own children to have a toolbox full of scriptures to use as needed, encouraging them to follow Him, and not get in the way of His will for their lives. I know there have been far too many times "my will" has gotten in the way of His progress in my life, and it happens when I have not spent time with Him.

Therefore, prepare your minds for action; be self-controlled; set your hope fully on the grace to be given you when Jesus Christ is revealed. (1 Peter 1:13 NIV)

Wherefore gird up the loins of your mind, be sober, and hope to the end for the grace that is to be brought unto you at the revelation of Jesus Christ. (1 Peter 1:13)

Janice: Deb, I can certainly relate to what you are saying. My number one goal as a parent has been to lead my children to Christ, teaching them to put their total trust and dependence upon Him. Our children learn attitude from us so when they ask for my opinion about something they are doing or planning to do, I use it as a teaching moment to ask them, "What does the Lord say?" or "Have you prayed and sought direction about this?" I want them to be dependent on me as a parent to a certain degree, but ultimately I want my children to hear the voice of God for themselves, listening to His will and direction for their lives. As we train our hearts and minds to actively listen to God, negativity becomes very limited because we are saying, "Lord, I trust You no matter what comes."

Deb: You know, Janice, our spiritual growth is a journey paved with difficulties and struggles that provide opportunity for a real attitude adjustment. Trusting God with my life and truly exercising faith that He is in control has done more for my attitude than believing I can adjust my own attitudes. He has shown me my very attitude belongs to Him, and I have proof He stands good on His promise.

But it was your own eyes that saw all these great things the LORD has done. (Deuteronomy 11:7 NIV)

Janice: You hit the nail on the head, Deb. If only we could adjust the lenses we view our lives through, we would see there is eternal hope. We don't have to see life through the dim light of negativity because there is the hope of building a peaceful and joyous life based on our relationship with Jesus Christ. We can learn to look at life through the eyes of the One who already has been there and knows the answers without being afraid of what lies ahead. In fact, Jesus Christ has already paid the price for you and me. We already know what the ending will be because God's Holy Word tells us, "I am Alpha and Omega, the beginning and the ending, saith the Lord, which is, and which was, and which is to come, the Almighty" (Revelation 1:8).

Deb: This is where faith and joy come into play. Honestly, Janice, we have to develop our faith which then is evident in our attitudes. "It is written 'I believed; therefore I have spoken.' With that same spirit of faith we also believe and therefore speak" (2 Corinthians 4:13 NIV). Our attitude of faith ultimately strengthens our faith in Him and in His ability to work through us. We can relax knowing that He has us in the palm of His hand. We can become joyous in knowing we are out of the driver's seat and He is now in control.

We should look for the joyous things in life. This is how our attitudes should be defined. "In God's presence is fullness of joy" (Psalm 16:11). It doesn't tell us everything will be perfect all the time. Beth Moore teaches a series on the book of James in which we are reminded of our responsibility to have a wise attitude when we are in the midst of trials and temptations. She brings to our attention James 1:2-4, "Consider it pure joy, my brothers, whenever you face trials of many kinds, because you know that the testing of your faith develops perseverance. Perseverance must finish its work so that you may be mature and complete, not lacking anything" (James 1:2-4 NIV).

Then if that doesn't do it, with her sweet voice ringing in the background of her unfeigned love for the King of kings, she directs us to one of Jesus' promises, "I tell you the truth, and you will weep and mourn while the world rejoices. You will grieve, but your grief will turn to joy" (John 16:20 NIV).

One of my favorite promises is, "In that day you will no longer ask me anything. I tell you the truth, my Father will give you whatever you ask in my name" (John 16:23 NIV). He didn't say, "If you ask, you will feel better." He didn't say if you ask for a new car, straight A's, help with your children or your marriage or your relationships at work; He said anything—whatsoever—it's all about your attitude and their attitude. He will provide, but you may not recognize the path He leads you down for the resolving and the answer to your prayer. We don't need to understand, we only need to believe.

Every time He answers my prayers I'm always amazed at how He answers, who He uses, and how it unfolds. I have said this for fifty years, **"His best is better than my best!"** He always provides resolutions that are superior to what I pray for.

27

Let this mind be in you which was also in Christ Jesus.
(Philippians 2:5 NKJV)

Your attitude should be the same as that of Christ Jesus.
(Philippians 2:5 NIV)

Only with Christ's help are we able to achieve the attitude and mindset that God wants us to have. For example, my attitudes are what I choose to think, feel and do based on my experiences in life. My attitude is the way I have grown accustomed to responding to people and circumstances, situations, problems, and personal pain. Godly attitudes are responding to people and situations the way God wants me to think, feel and act. Back twenty years ago I was "a bit ornery" according to my husband I used to have fun challenging those who came into my office to sell me a copier, computer, or office equipment. I actually embarrassed some of my staff beyond words. When a salesman approached me wearing a "Jesus First" button or later a "WWJD" bracelet, I would simply lay it on the line at the close of the meeting. Generally it went something like this:

"I am so glad to see you wearing the Jesus First Pin," I would say. "It amazes me your love of Christ. I, too, love Him supremely."

The salesman would feel that he had just closed the deal in that we shared a love for Christ.

I would then immediately say, "Because of your profession of faith and love, I hold you more accountable to be fair and honest with me. Every promise you made here today I will expect delivery of, and for you to abide by what you promised. The reason I say

28

this is I am tired of playing church. I am equally tired of Christian business luncheons where we claim to be different, and then don't act significantly different from non-Christians. If you are indeed a Christian and are wearing something that represents Him, it is my understanding that you live for Him, and will act to the best of your ability in doing nothing wrong. Can you live with this? If the answer is "yes," you can have my business."

What fun I had as I saw the look on their faces! The uncomfortable awkward moment for the team who worked with me, and the nervousness of the salesman struggling for an appropriate response in front of his manager happened in my office more times than I can count. Often though, if the deal was accepted, it was most beneficial for me in the form of the service I received.

Now back to the actual question Janice posed in the beginning of this chapter: "What is a godly attitude?" I believe it is an honest attitude, an attitude of **love**, an attitude where we try to see Christ in everyone, and hope that everyone sees Him in us. It is an attitude that doesn't find fault, nor is it jealous or envious. It is truly summed up in an attitude of **love**, much like the following passage from 1 Corinthians 13.

If I speak in the tongues of men or of angels, but do not have love, I am only a resounding gong or a clanging cymbal. If I have the gift of prophecy and can fathom all mysteries and all knowledge, and if I have a faith that can move mountains, but do not have love, I am nothing. If I give all I possess to the poor and give over my body to hardship that I may boast, but do not have love, I gain nothing. Love is patient, love is kind. It does not envy, it does not boast, it is not proud. It does not dishonor others, it is not self-seeking, it is not easily angered, and it keeps no record of wrongs. Love does not delight in evil but rejoices with the truth. It always protects, always trusts, always hopes, and always perseveres. Love never fails. But where there are prophecies, they will cease; where there are tongues, they will be stilled; where there is knowledge, it will pass away. For we know in part and we prophesy in part, but when completeness comes, what is in part disappears. When I was a child, I talked like a child; I thought like a child, I reasoned like a child. When I became a man, I put the ways of childhood behind me. For now we see only a reflection as in a mirror; then we shall see face to face. Now I know in part; then I shall know fully, even as I am fully known. And now these three remain: faith, hope and love. But the greatest of these is love. (1 Corinthians 13:1-13 NIV)

How Can I Develop a Godly Attitude?

Decide who you want to be in Christ Jesus. The world has changed so much, and most of us have unconsciously changed with it. We need to align our hearts and our minds to what is pleasing to Him.

- *Consider the movies you go to and the TV you watch. Is it helpful for building ourselves up in the Lord?*

- *Avoid pornography of all forms and have filters on your computers. Avoid anything else we have in our homes that are in conflict with the teachings of Christ. Also, we should be careful what we read. I have a pile of Christian books I intend to read this year, but less than I did last year, because my New Year's goal was to have one book read by the end of each month so that I can stay focused on the Word. Often times our Bibles lay unopened week after week.*

- *Refuse to listen to gossip. Do not participate in the activities of low return, and avoid the dirty jokes. "Nor should there be obscenity, foolish talk or course joking, which are out of place, but rather thanksgiving" (Ephesians 5:4 NIV).*

- *Do not listen to music which promotes sin and ungodliness.*

WOW! This living for Him is tougher than it seems. I think the most difficult things for people are to think about how they want to be, get a plan of action, and then move forward.

Over the past year I have practiced what I refer to as God-er-Cise.™ Most of my friends are tired of hearing about it. At first everyone was enthralled until they started realizing that I mean for all of us to do it in the gym or church. Imagine godly women praying like this together; talk about where there are two or more gathered together in His name. I am telling you if twenty women/men were to do this a couple of times a week, our attitudes, churches, schools, and ultimately our world would change, thus making the world a better place to be.

I have been fighting the call of offering God-er-Cise™ to churches in which the women/men could enjoy a time of stretching and gentle exercise while being led in worship, praise, and learning how to specifically pray. It would also encourage the art of meditating on the Lord with thanksgiving. There are many meditation exercises I have developed to remind me of how blessed I truly am.

I look at this like I do anything else, we are going to get the results we have always gotten if we continue to do the same things we have always done. Therefore, if we want to be more spiritual and more prayerful, we have to put the time in. The time we would spend learning a specific skill should be the same amount of time we should put in to developing our relationship with God.

On the front cover of Prevention Magazine there was an advertisement for a 20-minute miracle workout that targeted your trouble spots promising sculptured, and sexy hips. Now I am not saying I don't need that, because I do. However, in addition to my exercise for the heart, I want to learn to be more like Jesus and His amazing Grace. Therefore, I had better "hit the trouble spots" of my soul by falling on my face before Him and asking how to be like Him.

I can tell you that after one full year of doing this several times a week, my life has drastically changed and yours will, too. I have included an outline for you to use at home. However, this is not meant to replace your regular morning Bible reading and devotions.

GOD-er-CISE™

Since, then, you have been raised with Christ, set your hearts on things above, where Christ is seated at the right hand of God. Set your minds on things above, not on earthly things. For you died, and your life is now hidden with Christ in God. (Colossians 3:1-3 NIV)

GOD-er-CISE™ is a series of stretching and gentle exercises which encourage meditation and prayer on God. It is a time when we can come together as a family, group, church, or community to work on being healthier, and opening our hearts while developing a more Godly Attitude.

- Promotes repentance and fellowship with the Holy Spirit
- Helps to promote a healthy prayer life with others by promoting community togetherness while stretching, using gentle exercise. (Can be done from a chair or wheelchair, therefore includes everyone.)
- Encourages additional Bible Study time via book or tape in a group setting
- Encourages scripture memory work
- Places Psalms, hymns and spiritual songs upon our heart

- Fellowship with other believers
- Provides a safe place for meditation on the Word of God
- Reminds us to be thankful for the things God has done for me and others I know and pray for
- Gets us in touch with the holiness and perfection of God
- Encourages us to reflect on the beauty of Christ
- Allows us a redeeming worship service
- Allows us fellowship with Him
- The meaning/application of any specific passage of scripture
- Helps us to garner what God has just taught us or made us aware of and be thankful for it
- Helps us to discern the will of God for our life
- Celebrates salvation that we may not forget and take it for granted
- Reminds us to be thankful for the life He has freed us from

Janice: Deb I have enjoyed this new "God-er-cise" and our conversation immensely. Basically, we need to focus on Philippians 2:5 , giving our attitudes to Christ afresh each morning.

Chapter 2

Who Am I in Him?

And be not conformed to this world: but be ye transformed by the renewing of your mind, that ye may prove what [is] that good, and acceptable, and perfect, will of God. (Romans 12:2)

Janice: From the moment of my birth trouble has been a faithful companion. I shouldn't have survived! My mother was barely eighteen years old when she fell in love with my father and worshipped the ground he walked on, according to those who knew about their relationship. The two were inseparable and she did whatever she could to make him happy. Conceived from their troubled union, I was headed for trouble of my own. My mother grew up in an alcoholic family, unable to break free from the awful memories. My father was his mother's favorite son. She had lost an infant son and a still born previously, so she pampered him even when he was in the wrong. He never learned to stand on his own. As one might expect from such dysfunctional personality traits, my home life was a constant battle of wills between my parents. Unfortunately for me, my mother never came to terms with her issues and death seemed like a viable option.

Deb: Born the third child of an unhappy union, I entered the world with these welcoming words that hung in the air throughout my childhood, "Deb was an accident, and she was not planned." My mother was in her early forties when she delivered me that cold February day. I remember waiting for one of my parents to complete the sentence with, "We weren't expecting another child, but we are thrilled that you were born." Later they did soften it some by saying my sister was a straight "A" student, and Deb just likes to have fun. Somewhere along the way I started telling myself that everything was good. I don't know if this was my way of controlling my story or if it was a way of escaping the awful things that were going on in my home life. I just know that starting at an early age I was a very nervous and troubled child. I still recall my childhood doctor telling my parents that they shouldn't spank me because I had extreme anxiety. This was before anxiety was even talked about. Now enough about me! I need a break! Who are you?

Janice: *Who am I?* That's a question I know many of you have sought an answer to just like me. As many of you know, growing up can be a painful time, and for me it was just that way. My life was filled with a lot of fear and uncertainty. Growing up was a time of many doubts and insecurities about myself. My identity was one of those struggles. It was as if I lived outside of myself. I didn't know who I was nor was I in touch with my deepest thoughts or my own feelings. I don't even remember anyone asking how I felt, and it seemed no one was very interested in me at all. Maybe they did ask, I just don't remember. I was just like a little tumbleweed rolling in the wind. I kept everything locked inside and didn't express thoughts about anything. Maybe I just didn't have many thoughts or maybe I chose to keep them quiet. I don't know! As an adult though, I have had times of struggle sharing my real thoughts, and I've had to work very hard to find the problem when I feel out of sorts. Biting my nails is a bad habit I do subconsciously. When I do my husband will ask me what's wrong and I'll say, "I don't know." I really have to dig deep inside to find the source of my agitation.

Deb: You know, Janice, we come into this world peaceful, sweet smelling, pure, honest, and innocent. The world and its struggles, as we grow up have a way of shaping us. I find that "digging deep," as you put it, is painful, frustrating, and hopeless to a degree. It is our past that haunts us! Satan uses all of our pain and suffering to tear us down. We must look to God immediately when we find ourselves trying to understand our past pain. Biting your nails and becoming almost in a trance of the past must be taken to GOD . He mends our lives in steps as we grow in Him. Almost in bites size pieces or in baby steps we grow in Him. In other words it's a process and takes determination and diligence on our part to pursue Him. God has a way of working with us by these past hurts which allows us to find who we are in Him. We have a tendency to allow Him in just so far, and then we often take it from there. An example of this might be the way we ask our spouse or our children for their advice on the dress or shoes we've chosen to wear for a particular day. We ask earnestly, "Which one do you prefer? Or how does this look?" When we get an answer we aren't expecting, we storm off disappointed because it wasn't what we wanted to hear. Sometimes I feel we come to God with that same "attitude."

Janice: If only we could remain sweet and innocent. Deb, I remember the excitement I felt each time I became pregnant. The joy of having a little one was something I dearly cherished. When my son was finally born, his purity of being untouched by the world was so precious to me. But we all grow up and are faced with struggles that have the means to bring us down to the lowest of lows, or can lead us to Christ to dwell with Him in heavenly places, even in this life.

Deb: Life doesn't define us totally, although our struggles are many and our experiences do shape and mold us. When we surrender to our loving and faithful God, we do become the clay in the Potter's hand. I've known many people with countless adversities who trusted God completely for divine healing, and who are now magnificent disciples for His work. Often times our emotional development does take a long journey prior to the commitment of letting Christ in. With broken marriages and families falling apart, it does take a toll on kids and their development. I know it did for you and me.

Janice: I know it did, too. Unfortunately I think many of us are unknowingly ignorant in failing to see how families across our great nation are indeed falling apart. I believe we are equally ignorant of the influence a father has in the emotional development of his children. Somehow our society has made a mother's role more important than the father's role, but I think each role is equally important to a healthy family. The emotional investment of a father's time and energy creates a sense of security that causes his children to feel safe even when life's problems arise. They're not worried or concerned with their own safety because their father is the safety net that catches them when they falter. Think of those kids who look up to their dad, believing he is superman and nothing bad can happen when he is around. Well, an unloving father has the exact opposite effect making us feel vulnerable to outside forces. His very presence creates insecurities that lead to fear, rejection, bitterness, and a multitude of other bad feelings.

Fathers have the power to create security or insecurity just by the actions or behavior they display towards their children. I've known people, including myself, who associate God with the behaviors of their earthly father. My father was absent from my life, so I thought God was absent. I thought because my father didn't care about me, then God must not care about me.

Some people believe God is cruel looking down from heaven with a hammer because this is the way your earthly father treated you. When you made a mistake or an error you were beat down by words or with physical force. Those who have had a loving and accepting relationship with their father believe God is also loving and accepting.

It's a matter of perspective on our part. However, God isn't subject to our human perspective. He is a loving and accepting God, no matter how we were treated by our earthly fathers. He loves at all times. Does that mean He doesn't correct us when we disobey? Just like any loving father, our heavenly Father brings correction to those He loves. My own children are secure in their father's love because he is a loving and caring provider. They never question his love for them or their importance to me. This is a picture of God's love for us.

Deb: I think of how you wanted your children and recognized their innocence in comparison to God's love for us. We adults tend to think we're no longer children even though many times we still behave like children. If you don't believe me, consider your words the last time you argued with your spouse. The influence of a father you referred to opens up my own "war wounds." My dad was seldom available to me and certainly wasn't a provider. He abandoned us emotionally long before he physically left. I became a lost soul spending a great deal of time murmuring, "I don't get it." Life doesn't make sense, as you know. I have a big heart for teens and the pain they suffer. I guess you could say, "I get them."

Janice: One night, flipping through the television channels, I stopped on a station called *Animal Planet*. The program airing was called *Rogue Nature*, about young immature male elephants who, for reasons unknown, had been separated from the most important influence in their lives—their mothers, aunts, and sisters. Elephants live in a social order made up of mothers, aunts, daughters, sisters, and immature male and female elephants. The oldest female acts as the leader of their family, and under her guidance the adults teach the young. These young male elephants had no family unit, and grouped themselves with other male elephants, creating a "rogue" gang. Without boundaries or rules of conduct, they fought for dominance, running down rhinoceroses, and stabbing them to death with their tusks, then standing back as though they had done nothing. They rushed wildly into small villages, killing people, and fighting against any perceived threat. They were always looking for a fight.

Sitting there watching, I was reminded of the lost youth in our nation who act out in the same rebellious anger and disrespect. What I found so intriguing though was these male elephants had no parental guidance at all. They did whatever they wanted. Children and teenagers all over our great nation act out the same mischievous conduct, exhibiting rebellious behavior, and committing criminal acts as they look for the love and attention they were never given at home. Families make up the very foundation of any healthy society, and without a family's stability its youth will eventually be lost. Our families are slowly eroding away because children lack the steady parental guidance necessary for them to grow into emotionally healthy adults. Abandoning our children to the leadership and values of someone else weakens the family unit, our nation, and waters down our values.

Deb: My family unit was destroyed and blown up. Prior to its tragedy was the full-blown dysfunction that will take me and many others years to sort through. It is easier for me to get my head around it when I go back to my Bible. I always like to think we live in modern day Bible stories. The generational sins in most families are the same sins people in biblical times dealt with, too. Once you recognize that a certain sin has been in the family a long time, you begin to see its significance and the role it plays in our true spiritual condition. I keep saying, based on last year, I'm not sure if I even like my name. I feel I don't know the real me anymore. I sometimes tease and say I'm having an "identity crisis." When I opened my heart completely to Him, I recognized there were places in my heart which didn't belong to God. I refer to those places as "identity Christ-less" because I had not given them to God for healing. Now I can say, spiritually speaking, I know who I am and whose I am.

Janice: Webster's dictionary defines identity as "the relation established by psychological identification."[2] Naturally we identify with the person or persons we spend most of our time with. This helps in forming our identity. The role parents play in their children's development helps in forming their thoughts and who they eventually become. Children who have been abandoned or rejected identify with the first person who accepts them. It doesn't matter if that person is a gangster or a pastor; they gravitate towards the one who embraces them for who they are. We hear of young teens getting involved in gangs because of the sense of family they feel. Their loyalty to the gang is solidified because they feel a sense of purpose and of belonging.

The role of a mother is very important because she is the nurturing part of the family. Her voice is the first sound a baby hears in the womb. As her baby grows, he or she derives comfort from hearing her voice. The mother's mood also affects the baby, causing the child to be restless or peaceful. When a baby is born, the mother is usually the first to hold them, speaking words of comfort after a difficult delivery, or nursing the child at her breast, bringing comfort and security. How the mother feels about being pregnant is of great significance, too, because the child will experience love and acceptance, or rejection in the womb.

As the child grows, the mother is there to offer emotional support and comfort throughout their life. When the child scrapes their leg, she is there to kiss the boo-boo and dry the tears. She may cuddle, touch, or caress the child, letting them know she is there. Unfortunately, not all mothers are loving and kind. There are thousands of children born into families whose mothers aren't the nurturing type, and they have their own set of issues that limit them in giving of themselves. The struggle between mother and child brings so much pain and rejection because she fails to see the needs of her child to be loved and accepted by her. Some of you have mothers like I have just described. But God's Word says; "When my father and my mother forsake me, then the LORD will take me up" (Psalm 27:10). This means when you are abandoned, neglected and cast away, God will be to you both a father and a mother, and will receive you unto Himself. This passage of scripture has comforted me many times when I felt completely lost.

Identity Crisis in America

Janice: My husband and I still have three teenagers at home. We have always opened our home to their friends, and regularly one (or five) of their friends may just hang out or spend the night which has given me the opportunity to get to know them better. You see, part of my ministry has been to the young men who walk through the front door of my home. Some of them come from broken homes, some have relationship problems, while others just want to be loved and accepted. I have been privy to some of their problems because they have confided in me, and I've taken the opportunity to share Christ with them. I get what is going on with them. Sadly, they are going through an identity crisis of huge proportions along with the other countless teenagers who find themselves in the same situations. The struggles they face are more serious than ever, and the questions they have about their life and what their future holds are yet to be determined.

Unfortunately, the mass media are all too willing to provide guidance, and eagerly provide earthly sensual wisdom to their problems because parents are apparently too busy to see the warning signs. Parents, we are failing our children because we simply are too busy to give them the time and energy needed to provide the loving guidance necessary for happy healthy children. When kids lack loving parental guidance it's easy for them to embrace false concepts of individuality. Sadly, our children watch way too much television with its influencing lies that teach them sexual promiscuity and suggest alternative approaches to God.

Parents, wake up! Time is getting short and the opportunity to reach your children is slipping away. The time to reach them will soon be gone. Don't wait until it's too late.

Deb: I couldn't agree more. We must teach our children to **follow** Christ and the teachings of His Holy Word. Just recently, I encouraged our fifteen-year-old daughter to pray for God's will in her own life regarding where He wants her to go to school next year. Without manipulating her as a parent, because I think I know where she should be, I joined her in praying, fasting, and seeking His will. I watched God as He orchestrated the answer, and realized it was as much about me regarding my faith as it was about her and His direction for her life. I stand amazed at His teachings when we are open to praying and selflessly seeking His will for the outcome.

Janice: As a parent I see the struggles kids are faced with today, and I've wondered why they are drawn away from what's true and right. Why are they embracing lies? What are the factors contributing to their rapid descent into deception? I believe the factors are many. For one, our society encourages sex outside of marriage by offering condoms to kids in school.

According to ETWN News, A Global Catholic Network, "The U.S. National Vital Statistics Report for April 2010, produced by the

Center for Disease Control's National Center for Health Statistics, said the number and percent of births to unmarried women each increased to historic levels. About 40.6 percent of children were born to an unmarried mother in 2008, an increase from 39.7 percent the previous year."[3] So we see that many more children are born out of wedlock than ever before in history.

Drug abuse is another trap society is beginning to accept as normal. There are even some who lobby our politicians in Washington to make illegal drugs lawful. Another contributing factor is both parents work outside the home and children are left with babysitters, in daycare centers, or return from school to an empty house. Parents are so busy providing physically for their children they forget to provide for them spiritually. In so doing, we invite the influence of others whose ideas of God and the world around us may differ from our own beliefs. I know many single moms struggle hard to keep their family together. At one time I was a single mom and I understand how hard it is to leave your kids in the care of someone else. I know from personal experience when I had to leave my oldest son in someone else's care and the difficulty in doing that. Many days I found it hard to work because I worried all day about him.

I know many of you are torn as well. The responsibility of providing, loving, and disciplining rests on your shoulders alone and certainly can take an emotional toll. Sadly, our homes are breaking down and falling apart at an unbelievable rate because parents are too embattled with one another to stop and think about the effect their relationship and actions are having on their children. Our children are the most vulnerable and the least considered in our society as well as in the family. Seldom do we stop to consider how our actions are affecting them. Instead of working our relationships out, we're opting out and leaving our precious children with emotional scars they don't know how to fix.

So now our kids are gravitating towards false concepts and ideas, hoping to find something or someone to believe and hold on to when their emotional needs are simply not being met at home. Not only do our kids attend schools to educate them, but activist teachers are taking the opportunity to teach their own liberal views because Mom and Dad aren't paying attention and have dropped their spiritual responsibilities into someone else's lap. It's becoming clearer that the absence of a father in the home creates a lack of security, protection, and safety. A loving father provides much needed stability for a happy home. When both parents are in the home children's security is even greater. Without a father's protection, any wave of doctrine or idea will be accepted more easily as truth.

A loving father knows how to instruct his children in truth, and gives them something to believe in. Our youth wander about blindly accepting whatever appears to be right, but the watchful eye of a loving father will deter them from accepting any idea masquerading as truth. Does that mean we won't experience times of rebellion, disappointment, and misfortune? Of course not! Being human guarantees we're going to face troubles at some point in our lives, but the guidance of a loving father will determine how well we cope and overcome the obstacles that lie ahead.

Many of you will argue that a mother's influence is the same as a father's influence. I can only answer you by saying that in God's creation of the family, there is an order He put into place for our protection. When we follow that order there is peace, but when we step outside that order, chaos ensures and trouble soon follows. I would rather do it God's way and have peace in my family, than argue about my ideas of which I think to be right.

Deb: *I often wonder who am I that You, Lord Jesus are so fond of me?* I have had to control everything since I was a very young child. Controlling my life was how I coped with what was happening to me. I convinced myself that I was in control and no one could hurt me. That is how I survived years of abuse. I am so blessed that as a young-ster, Christ held me in the palm of His hand and protected me. Think of our lives as a book with the final chapter not having been written. Amen! Yes, Amen! How He hears my prayers, how He thinks of me, and sings over me. God's love is amazing, truly amazing. Our friend-ship runs deep and I am so pleased to call Him my friend.

My dad never answered questions. There was always an air of secrecy about him in everything.

I must have been around the age of eighteen when he said to me in front of my girlfriends, "Your mother was a good woman."

Feeling a bit braver than normal, I responded with, "Oh, really, why did you leave us then?"

I can recall that was the only time I had the nerve to question his authority or question him so boldly.

He simply said in a secret tone, "It was for the best for you and your sister."

"What do you mean, dad?" I inquired.

He responded, "Someday you'll understand."

"What's up with this kind of endless secrecy or non-responsive behavior," I thought, "when I deserved so much more?"

He always told me he gave up the bottle the day I was born and never had another drop after that.

My first carnal response was always, "Well, you didn't give up the character defects did you?"

I was still so very angry, and besides, I knew he was lying. On more than one occasion I saw him succumb to the bottle. He was one of those who went on binges for months at a time. It could be one month or it could be three months before you heard from him. After his funeral his wife gave me a picture album, and told me she wanted me to have it. I remember looking through the album. The pictures were made during the period of time just after he left us the last time. Many of them revealed he was still tipping the bottle. It broke my heart as it confirmed my suspicions that he had been dishonest the whole time. It still pains me to say it now. Why does it still hurt so badly? I want the story to be different and it just isn't. It is what it is.

My father was a very controlling, angry, and resentful man. He feared death, and he drilled into my head daily what I was to do if he had a heart attack. He had his first heart attack at the age of forty. After that, the fear of a second heart attack controlled his every waking thought. He was extremely selfish, mean, and manipulative, yet so charming to those who were outside the family. My mother told my sister and me not to blame him because he simply had no conscience. At the time that meant nothing other than she had a huge heart. Now it means a lot more, and her opinion means a lot more. She was right! He didn't seem to care deeply about anyone, especially his daughters.

My father took me to the barber shop to get my hair cut like a boy. He encouraged me not to wear a shirt when I was ten or eleven years of age. He always wanted a boy, but seemed happy he had made me into a boy. He told me dirty jokes and I can remember being so embarrassed my face would burn red, paling over with embarrassment.

Janice: Deb, today I cried for you because I understood all too well the hurt your heart was feeling. I so much understood the struggle. Hearing the quiver in your voice and the pain in your words, my heart hurt for you. I am very well acquainted with the feeling of not knowing my father, too. To my knowledge my father wasn't an alcoholic, but he does have his hang ups, and has always been extremely secretive and suspicious of others, yet very charming when necessary. He doesn't share personal things about his life with any of us children so we are left to wonder. I really don't know him well although I see him periodically. We seldom talk because the bond between parent and child never developed. I probably see him once a year and we don't talk over the phone. I have four sons in whom he hasn't developed a relationship with either. If by some chance he does come to see us, it's because he is on his way somewhere else and just happened to be in the area. Even sadder is the fact he has never shared with us anything about our mother. I have lived most of my life knowing very little about her except for what little I remember.

Like you, Deb, my father instilled in me the notion that I was worthless, although he never spoke the words "you're worthless" to me. It wasn't what he did that made me feel worthless, but what he didn't do that caused me the most pain. The love and approval I needed from him never came. I couldn't rely on him to meet my emotional needs because he was never around and there was too much distance between us. I rarely saw him or even spoke to him. But when I did, he was always in a hurry to be someplace else. Usually his plans were to play music with his bluegrass buddies leaving little time for us to be with him, so we spent most of our visit with our grandparents.

You see, a father's absence creates an emotional void opening wide the door for relationships that are unhealthy and unwholesome. A daughter especially needs an emotional bond with her father, yearning to have his approval and acceptance. In its absence, she innocently gravitates towards the first man willing to give her the attention she longs for. In essence choosing a man much like her father who is emotionally unavailable and repeating the same pattern of harmful behavior. Sadly, she willingly exchanges the sacred for the vile to fill the emptiness she feels inside, and then afterwards she is consumed with remorse because of what she's done. Then the pattern repeats itself again. If anyone were to ask her why she does this, she would tell them she doesn't know and she doesn't want this kind of life for herself. Neither can she explain the yearning for love that pushes her to the edge of insanity. Underneath the surface are the unmet emotional needs that have compelled her to continue down this destructive path in search of something she feels she can never have.

We look down on women who seem to be sexually driven. We fail to see that behind the promiscuity is a wounded individual who is looking for the love and acceptance of her own father. The young women in our society dress loosely hoping to gain attention from the opposite sex because they never had the attention of a father. I'm forty-nine years old, and I've never had my father's approval because he never took the time or made the effort to know me. We must educate fathers on this subject in order to raise young women who are Godly wives and mothers, impacting the family for Christ-centeredness.

Fathers, I believe it's time you took your rightful place in your daughter's life. Don't you agree?

I idolized him simply because he was my father. Faithfully I wrote letters declaring my love and devotion, but eventually I understood all of his promises were empty. The realization that he would never come for me was quite sobering, and I eventually stopped writing. Soon my heart was filled with bitter angry feelings, the love and hope I once felt were gone. So I blocked out thoughts and feelings associated with him to avoid feeling any pain. All I ever wanted was his love, but he couldn't even do that. I cried myself to sleep at night, the feelings of emptiness and loneliness eating away at my heart.

As a result, I was immature emotionally for a girl my age. Somewhere along the way I had given up, and built a hard outer shell around my once pliable heart. My relationships with others were affected, too, and I would sometimes lash out in heated anger at the least amount of internal pain or prodding. I couldn't even talk about how I felt or why I felt the way I did. I was completely out of touch with myself. There were simply no words to describe my broken condition. Sadly, no one else could explain it either. I was invisible because I didn't exist.

Deb: Becoming more spiritual doesn't have a chance in our country today. We as a people are too busy being busy. Things are changing and they're changing fast due to our preoccupation with life and all it has to offer. We do not have the allegiance to Him that we should. Just like the flight I am on right now, looking around I see a society who is too busy for Christ. We crowd Him out. People busy themselves just like the adult male in his 30's sitting next to me on the plane today playing intense games on his phone. He is a well-built guy, who takes much of our space as he sways back and forth breathing heavily, mastering his skill at blocking out life.

Now don't get me wrong. I have played games and found them very addictive, therefore, I have taken them off my phone. I have replaced the games with spiritual helps such as an icon for Sarah Young, my favorite daily devotional. I have listened to the whisper in my ear from the Master who leads me along the still waters and restores my soul. It is my time to be busy with Him.

All scripture is inspired by God and is useful to teach us what is true and make us realize what is wrong with our lives. It corrects us when we are wrong and teaches us to do what is right (Timothy 3:16 NLT)

God uses it to prepare and equip His people to do every good work. I feel like God's call on my life makes so much sense, and the deliverance of His words through His scripture was written just for me. We can do a lot of things but we can't have other gods before Him; whether those gods are our spouses, our children, our work, our sports, our hobbies, and even our own peace seeking mission. It is not about **us** or about **them**. We can't help them, but there is one who can, our **Lord Jesus Christ**. So the best thing we can do for ourselves and our peace seeking minds is to study His Word, ensuring our children do the same, otherwise we have come no further than those whom He tried to teach when He walked this earth. Isn't it a hoot that I have lived 57 years to tell you that simple truth?

In the airport ladies' room, I noticed the cleaning attendant was singing and praising God. Some travelers rolled their eyes as she shared her child like faith as if she was crazy, while others spoke with her about God. Some tipped her, others said that's all she wanted and walked swiftly away. But God told me to share with her how sweet and refreshing her message was. It is my belief our society is certainly crowding Him out without realizing it. I feel we must support anyone, any place talking out loud about our Savior although it is odd to hear. I do what He tells me. If I don't then I am persecuting Christians and disappointing Him with my lack of involvement. There is coming a day when we as Americans will need to take our country back on the principles that it was founded upon and be willing to stand up for God.

You hear every day ways atheists are able to get God out of something valuable and important to our children. We have managed to continue to roll over and play dead as they continue to change the America we once knew. We were so blindsided back in the '60s when Madelyn Murray O'Hair was successful in having prayer taken out of school. We are astonished that in 2012 we continue to say to each other, "We should really work to get that ruling overturned." Now come on, are we true Christian's or are we so uncomfortable with our beliefs that we can't speak up?

We are repeating history and are no different than those in the early church who turned to other gods and were reprimanded by God. Are we as a society going down the tubes because we idly stand by and watch, not speaking up for God and our beliefs? If so, we aren't any different than anyone else who complains about the shape our country is in. What are we doing about it? I feel like we are youngsters in school with the defeat of peer pressure so strong on us that we can't speak up. We look around and see individuals doing great work, but if we were asked to all come together, would our puffed up ego allow us to join together collectively and create something that would work, or are we willing to be individually defeated? We will stand together when we all finally get it, but not by our individual work or anything we do. It is by His Grace that we are able to do good things for Him.

Janice: Deb, I have been saying the exact same things for many years. There is an over abundance of lies and propaganda being pumped into our society on a daily basis. Believers regularly feast on these untruths and the Church has slowly been put to sleep. The Book of Matthew teaches us about the ten virgins who were supposed to be making themselves ready to meet the bridegroom. Instead, they slumbered and slept. In other words they were busying themselves with the worries of life and weren't paying attention to the time at hand. As you know only five of the virgins were ready when the bridegroom came. The other five missed their opportunity. We as believers are going to miss Him if we continue to blindly accept the lies being thrown at us.

Don't get me wrong. I'm aware that all societies and cultures before us have had to deal with the same kinds of lies, but there were no media outlets or electronic devices in which they could receive instantaneous information like we have now. It took a while for those lies to infiltrate a whole society. Now it just a matter of turning on the television or surfing the web and we are able to get information at the speed of sound. Falsehoods and lies are floated by the media and heralded as truth every single day. Yet it seems no one is interested in challenging their efficacy. Instead of questioning the bases of their validity, we choose instead to embrace them without further challenge.

One example of a lie that has been perpetuated over and over is the idea that "there are many pathways to God" or that "God doesn't even exist." I bring this up because of all the lies we choose to believe, this is the most damning lie of all. The eternal consequences of this one lie will doom anyone who blindly accepts it. In John 10:1 Jesus warns us, "Verily, verily, I say unto you, He that enters not by the door into the sheepfold, but climbs up some other way, the same is a thief and a robber." Some of you will passionately argue, "I don't believe in the virgin birth, death, burial, and resurrection of Jesus Christ."

Each of us is entitled to believe what we choose, but we aren't entitled to our own truth. The truth remains that Christ came regardless of anyone's beliefs. Being the mere humans that we are, we certainly have no influence over truth because truth belongs only to God. Intuitively man knows there is a higher power although he may never admit it. False gods are the result of man's futile attempts to find God in his life. In so doing he creates a false god that reflects his own ideas and thoughts of what he wants his god to be. As long as we hold to our belief that God doesn't exist or that there are many gods to choose from, we'll remain spiritually blind and in our sin, without hope of the healing we seek to find. No other god can claim miracle healing power—only Jesus Christ the Son of God. I will say it again, "There is only one way to God and that is through His son Jesus Christ." Those who believe we can be saved through other means are damned by the lie they believe.

Deb: We are fragile, broken, tattered, and torn remnants who seek to be more like Him. Overall, I think we, as Christians, wish we could be more like Him—only without having to suffer our upbringing and tragedies. But the truth is that we must walk where He walked. We must be delivered from our sin and iniquity before we can have a clue as to where He is calling us and what He has in store for each of us. God molds and makes us into His image when we remove the walls we put between us and Him. Remember there are no limits or boundaries to what He can do or how He will ultimately use us. Who we are in Christ determines our willingness to be used by Him. So we must stand firmly planted on His promises, and open ourselves to the discovery of who we are by placing our past, present, and future in the capable hands of His divine will. I don't know about you, but I find that exciting!

So basically we are back to discovering, "Who I am in Him and how do I get there from here?" First, we give ourselves completely to Him—not holding anything back. Secondly, we blanket ourselves in His love, grace, and mercy, and lay aside our defenses, dreams, and desires. Thirdly, we open our hearts for a total cleansing and rebirth, going back to the purity we were born with. Lastly, we ask Him to heal the broken pieces of our life, allowing Him to direct our footsteps along the path He chooses. In this we will find who we are in Him.

The question is, "Who are we now in Christ?" A good barometer to live by is a saying my husband loves and has taught to young people for years;

Watch your thoughts; they become words.

Watch your words; they become actions.

Watch your actions; they become habits.

Watch your habits; they become character.

Watch your character; it becomes your destiny.

(Author Unknown)

If we were living by this creed, we would be closer to being in touch with who He desires for us to be.

Chapter 3

Open Your Heart and Allow Christ to Heal You

I will not die but live, and will proclaim what the LORD has done. (Psalm 118:17 NIV)

Deb: In Chapter 13 of Luke, you may be familiar with the account of the old woman whom Jesus healed. Jesus was teaching in one of the synagogues on the Sabbath when a woman who had been incapacitated and crippled by a spirit for eighteen years came in. Jesus called to her and told her, "Woman, you are set free from your infirmity" (Luke 13:12 NIV). Then in verse 13 He touched her and immediately she straightened up and praised God. I believe that Jesus is the same yesterday, today, and forever more. Therefore, I know without a shadow of a doubt that this Bible story is true and real. I also know that Jesus has been in the process of healing me for many years, and that my broken heart was the root of my sickness.

The woman was healed and praised God for it. God received all the glory for her healing. Her story provides **hope** just as we pray this book will provide healing and hope for its readers.

I hope you do not get me mixed up with the "old lady" in the Bible story because I am only fifty-seven, and I plan to be young for a little while longer in that God has truly healed me of many things. I have had a plethora of medical problems, from the diagnosable to the un-diagnosable, real or imagined. I have suffered since I was eighteen years old. I look back and feel as though God was trying to heal me all along, but listening is not a strength I possess in my flesh. Healing has taken me a lot longer than either God or I had hoped for or planned. I have suffered from low white cell count and arthritic symptoms for years with many other significant symptoms of Lupus. I have been diagnosed as ANA negative Lupus which pleased some of my doctors and perplexed others. I have had excellent health care providers whom have become my friends on a quest to get Deb well. None of them to my knowledge felt that I had emotional or mental issues.

I have a history of mixed connective tissue disease, Lupus, seizures, Sjögren's, Relapsing Polychondritis, and Reynaud's disease. I have suffered from neurological, endocrine, cardiology, blood pressure, rheumatologic, and gastrointestinal ailments. I have a brain tumor in the front left cortex which causes seizures, and I have been a very sick gal many times in my life. I do believe that many of these things were consummated by my ailing heart and

61

soul. I am not saying that I am a hypochondriac nor am I suggesting misdiagnosis because this is "real stuff." I do believe however, that many were caused from holding on to the pain and agony of childhood trauma. My mantra of praise and healing is taken from Psalms and I do feel like singing it.

Praise the LORD, O my soul; all my inmost being, praise his holy name. Praise the LORD, O my soul, and forget not all his benefits—who forgives all your sins and heals all your diseases, who redeems your life from the pit and crowns you with love and compassion, who satisfies your desires with good things so that your youth is renewed like the eagles.
(Psalm 103:1-5 NIV)

In sitting down to rest this afternoon, I glanced over and noticed several magazines on my reading table. They must have been allowed into my shopping cart with the realization that I need to shed a few pounds. As I examine the covers, the article titles jump off the page. My heart pounds as I peruse the pages because between them hope is offered: "slim down secrets, fat fighters that work, you'll be thinner by dinner, a flat belly in 5 days!" STOP! I believe, I believe! I smile and say to myself, if only we were more conscious of our souls, which require our utmost care and an internal examination. The titles might read, "Build me up, strengthen me, feed me from the Word of God, don't let me atrophy or waste away!" Have you ever seen a person's arm or leg after coming out of a cast? The muscles often times have atrophied or wasted away if you will.

There will be a physical reckoning of that one arm or leg which is now smaller than the other. I see our souls much the same with the obvious lack of care we provide, wasting away, shriveling up, tired, weary, unused, glossed over, and forgotten.

Janice: Deb, back forty-five years ago when you and I were both youngsters, America was a different place and time. Families centered their lives on God and the church was the nucleus of almost every community. It was commonplace to see people attending church regularly, and making an effort to live by a set of moral standards that now are nothing more than a distant memory. Today we profess Christianity, however; we have relegated God to an empty room in our hearts whose door is seldom opened until trouble comes our way. I find it deplorable that the only time we want God in our lives is when we're in trouble. How sad God must feel knowing He's only called upon when afflictions trouble us. Honestly, I think we are too concerned with the temporary. We are so obsessed with having things that we crowd Him out of our lives in exchange for the temporal. We're substituting the eternal for things that are fading. Can we only find satisfaction in what we own or who we think we are?

But lay up for yourselves treasures in heaven, where neither moth nor rust doth corrupt, and where thieves do not break through nor steal. (Matthew 6:20)

Deb: Wow, Janice, what a coincidence that we are talking about this. My two youngest children and I have been having meaningful conversations during our meal time in which we challenge one another in conversation centered on God. We have to center our conversations on things that don't cost money; it can't be about technology, games, or expensive items of worldly interest. Try it! It is almost impossible to have this kind of conversation without quoting scripture or referencing what God wants in our lives. Next time you're out to dinner, pay attention to both young and old on their cell phones or handheld electronic devices. Although our culture is technologically advanced, I wonder how they would react if they were having a face-to-face conversation for an interview or conflict within their marriage.

Janice: Deb, that would be a difficult challenge because too much of our concern is directed towards having more and more of everything that money can buy; bigger homes, fancier cars, fabulous vacations, the perfect body, prestige, and many other things we hang our hopes on. What happened to God being the center of our lives? I sometimes chuckle about people's obsessions with having the "perfect body." Of course, we all know there is no such thing, yet we strive to achieve the impossible. Huge amounts of time and energy are wasted at the gym, lifting weights, dancing to the beat of Zumba, running the treadmill, and narcissistically staring at oneself in the mirror to see how well our exercise program is working. We idolize and worship our sensual appetites with a self-inflated ego of self-centeredness thinking this is all there is to life.

I'm not arguing that we shouldn't take care of ourselves by exercising and eating properly because our bodies are the temple of the Holy Spirit, but so much focus and attention will not matter in the end. My husband often jokes with me over my illusion of achieving the "perfect body" and says, "When you die, I'm going to put on your tombstone — 'She finally lost all that weight'." The point is that ultimately streamlining my figure will not matter because this body of clay is going back to where it came from — the dirt. Scripture tells those who focus on the physical fleshly appetites that destruction awaits them in the end.

Whose end [is] destruction, whose God [is their] belly, and [whose] glory [is] in their shame, who mind earthly things. (Philippians 3:19)

Deb: There is absolutely nothing wrong with having self-help around us. Some may be enjoying a book regarding how to eat well, live well, prevent heart disease, live longer, change this, change that, and change... I think carnally speaking they are providing much needed assistance. I do believe, however, that our souls are crying out! We need to restore, redeem, revive, relieve, and reconcile our spiritual selves. As I used to speak to folks in the work place, "Do a check up, from the neck up, and stop your stinkin' thinkin'." My new love is to open your heart, allowing Him to examine and redeem all of the broken pieces. As children we sang a song in church about broken pieces that related to allowing Christ to mend us.

Pick up the broken pieces and bring them to the Lord
Pick up the broken pieces trust in His Holy Word
He will put you back together and make your life complete
Just place the broken pieces at the Saviors feet (author paraphrase)

The song finishes with, "He made a body out of clay." Our bodies are really just clay vessels to guide us through this life journey. As a wonderful friend puts it, "Our bodies are our radar to tell us when something isn't right, or that certain things make us feel uncomfortable." We must listen and pay attention to that gut feeling, which is another reference for our soul. There is a reason for our clay existence, but in all honesty that carnal body needs less help than our souls.

Janice: Our passion for stroking our worldly sensual appetites not only hinders us from the importance of building Godly character, but deflects us from our real purpose which is to "glorify God and enjoy Him forever" as quoted in the Christian Catechisms. Chris Sligh, one of American Idol's Christian contestants, sings a song titled *"Empty Me."* The following chorus sums up the importance of emptying ourselves into Christ:

Empty me of the selfishness inside-
Every vain ambition and the poison of my pride-
And any foolish thing my heart holds to-
Lord empty me of me so I can be filled with You- Chris Sligh

This is my prayer for myself and mankind that we empty ourselves of all vanity, selfish ambition, and pride. In so doing we will change the world. Changing ourselves to become more like Christ is what holds eternal value, making us more acceptable unto God. Our families will be healthier and happier in every way, making the world a better place for everyone. My friend, we have only one life to live, and our goal should be to prepare ourselves to meet our Maker. "For what shall it profit a man, if he shall gain the whole world, and lose his own soul?" (Mark 8:36). We all will spend an eternity in the joyful bliss of God's presence or in an eternal place of damnation. We have a choice today—what will your choice be?

Deb: God tells us in Jeremiah 29:13 that when we seek Him we will find Him. I believe it so strongly that I not only want to offer it to you, I tend to want to push it down your throats. I'm so thrilled with the new me! Because of Him I am a newly redeemed creature. I love Him supremely and finally I get it that true spiritual healing is a moment by moment walk with Him. I refer to Him even in the slightest decisions. You are saying, "Well, I do that!" I thought I did, too. I've been serving Him over forty years, but it was only this past year that He revealed to me my pain and suffering. Ultimately His desire is to heal me.

My suffering, I believe, stemmed from what has been called auto-immune diseases. I have been burdened many years with aches, pains, and true diagnosable ailments. I have had a plethora of health problems which ran my physical being into the ground. However, I was never satisfied that I was sick, and I longed for answers, equally researching and praying for God's healing. I knew that I was suffering but felt in my soul something was amiss. I have recently been studying Psychoneuroimmunology (PNI). This is the study of the interaction between psychological processes and the nervous system and immune system of the human body. In other words, the long term effects of stresses on our bodies.

I am amazed at all the people who are misunderstood not misdiagnosed. Consider the role of the patient who presents to the physician multiple complaints, waiting for him or her to wave a magic wand and make it all better. I read an article yesterday in the newspaper while sitting in the doctor's office suggesting that physicians request essays from their patients to help assist them in better understanding what is going on in their bodies. What a novel idea—listening, truly listening, and hearing the cries of the soul. In today's times, with the enormous responsibilities of physicians, and the changes in the healthcare field, it is nearly impossible to hear the patient. My hope is that someone will run with this concept, hire people who enjoy listening and writing to better assist these folks get their medical stories out so that doctors can help them.

I have talked with many people who have been written off by physicians who think they are crazy, or because they have "more serious" patients to attend to. I am so blessed to have been listened to and treated with the utmost respect by wonderful doctors who took me seriously. But at the same time, I was so blocked! I had so much to say but couldn't say it until now. If we are doing this book for anyone **it is you, the one** who hurts so deeply and can't find the strength or words to "come out" with your pain and troubles. There are actual links between immunity and stress; there is scientific research on how the brain and immune system works in conjunction with each other. A helpful book on this subject is *The Self-Healing Personality* written by Dr. Howard S. Friedman. I made a good attempt of exposing mind over matter in my first book, *Attitude Therapy*.

As always there is more to the story, and that is where the rubber meets the road in the Book of John, which says; "He that believeth on me, as the scripture hath said, out of his belly shall flow rivers of living water" (John 7:38). My favorite scripture for healing is in the book of Proverbs and it says; "Trust in the Lord with all your heart and lean not to your own understanding. In all your ways acknowledge Him, and He will make your paths straight" (Proverbs 3:5-6).

Janice: Deb, you are right! Following Christ wherever He leads is a deliberate act on our part. Sometimes He leads us in ways that make little sense at all, but learning to trust, we are able to lay aside our own fears and doubts knowing His ultimate desire is to bring us to the place of healing. We often question why healing is so painful. When a person has a third degree burn, the pain of healing is far worse than when the burn first happened. All three layers of the epidermis are deeply affected making it a serious life-threatening trauma. Healing requires skin to be graphed from other areas of the body and put on the burned areas to replace what was burned up. So not only is the burn victim having to deal with the pain of the burn itself, but they must also endure the pain of having their skin removed from other areas of their bodies. This makes the process of healing slower and much more painful, causing extensive scarring of the skin.

Our emotional pain is much the same way in that it affects us down to the very core of our being leaving years of emotional scars on our hearts, minds, and souls. When God begins the healing process on our hearts, the pain I think is worse than the original hurt we encountered. How can that be? Because when emotional hurt and pain are left unattended, the roots of bitterness and unforgiveness sprout, growing their roots deep inside our souls making them difficult to uproot. That's why there is so much suffering emotionally when we decide we're ready to confront and face our issues. We must face the years of painful scars and pull out by the root their cause. For some of us it takes a long time and for others, they get it quickly. I think healing took me longer because I had to emotionally process what was happening to me. I had to prepare my heart to receive inner healing.

Deb: The chest and its cavity protect our internal organs by providing a suit of armor. The thoracic cage is formed by the ribs, sternum and vertebra, and prevents damage to the heart and lungs. Our hearts are complex and involved, although well protected. My suit of armor (self-protection) extended down to my belly button and completely around to the spine. I am speaking of my defense that was much like an armadillo shell which I engaged for self-protection. I have come to know this through much needed counseling. I also know how our hearts and minds engage to protect the child within us. It is as complex as a finely woven piece of linen or fabric. Imagine taking one thread in a silk scarf and pulling it. Can't you see the material bunching up, drawing together in a fit of wrinkles and entanglement? So it is with our souls which is the very fiber of our beings. This hopefully lays the groundwork for how intricate we are and how complicated the healing is. It is my firm belief that, without God, we could never fully heal the brokenness of our hearts.

Above all else, guard your heart, for it is the wellspring of life. (Proverbs 4:23 NIV)

King Solomon tells us that above all, guard your heart. He doesn't say if you have a little extra time or if other things don't push you for time. He says **guard it**! It is the wellspring of life, and affects our words, thoughts, and actions. A man's heart describes who he is. "For he is the kind of man who is always thinking about the cost. 'Eat and drink,' he says to you, but his heart is not with you" (Proverbs 23:7 NIV). This reminds me we should be filling our hearts with scriptures, promises, hope, and love. It is like a new computer. We sit down, open the bubble wrap, smell the newness, and plug it in. If we begin surfing the web and pour porn, trash, and junk in our hearts that is what will come out of our mouths. It truly isn't more complicated than that. Our hearts are constantly under attack from the enemy. He wants us to eat fast food, drink pop, and not exercise because when our hearts are unhealthy everything else is complicated and compromised. We don't have the energy to minister to others, our careers fail, and our children and spouses suffer as they watch us become ill. Take care of your heart and health. Expose your heart to God daily so that He may examine and heal it. Disciplining ourselves to study His Word will keep our hearts healthy, alive, and free.

It is said that scientists today are researching the capabilities of our hearts and the possibility that our hearts think. We know scriptures describe our heart thinking, so why would we believe anything else? Recently while researching our hearts and scriptures, I came across a very interesting article and I'd like to share pieces of it with you.

A number of years ago, Claire Silvia from Boston, USA, had a heart transplant. Pretty soon she started to experience strange things. "It was like a whole new rhythm, a whole new feeling," she explains. And when a journalist asked her, soon after the transplant, what she now wanted most in the world, the words "I'd die for a cold beer right now!" suddenly popped out of her mouth, much to her embarrassment and surprise – she didn't previously even like beer! "Little by little," she says, "other things started happening until I was convinced I was living with the presence of another within me." Claire not only noticed changes in her tastes, her pref-erences for foods and drinks, but even in her handwriting. All she knew of the person who had donated her/his heart was that he was a young man who died in a motorcycle accident. Strict confidentiality rules mean that organ recipients aren't allowed to know the details of their donor. Then one night she dreamed of her donor and the name "Tim L" popped into her mind. The next day she rang her transplant co-ordinator and told her about the changes she had experienced, and asked her if her donor's name was in fact Tim L. There was silence on the other end of the phone, and then the co-ordinator said, "Please don't pursue this." It turned out that her donor's name was in fact Tim Lamarand.

Gary Schwartz, a professor of psychology and psychiatry at Yale University has developed a theory that could explain how the heart learns and remembers. Schwartz points out that all that is required for a system to be able to learn is that it has dynamic feedback: the outputs feed back to the inputs. Any such system that has feedback can learn. As the brain and the heart have feedback—both through neurons and through the blood-stream—the heart can in theory learn. Today we laugh at the notion that our hearts could be intelligent, we see them as basic pumps. A pump doesn't have thoughts, emotions and memories. But perhaps we don't know as much as we think we do.[4]

But rejoice that you participate in the sufferings of Christ, so that you may be overjoyed when his glory is revealed. (1 Peter 4:13 NIV)

I praise God that I was the victim and not the predator. I praise God the way my life has turned out because it could have ended up ridiculously complicated. I could have taken many routes in life to ease my suffering, and early on I did. But *Praise God*, He claimed me by the time I was nineteen years old. I awoke one morning with the decision to follow Christ or suicide. I truly found myself in so much misery and pain that I knew it was one or the other. I had played church long enough. I poured the liquor down the sink and flushed the pot and cocaine down the toilet. I feel that God took such a loving grip on my heart that enabled me to go forward for Him. I can recall having slip ups, the drugs and alcohol were just helping me to bury the pain deeper by complicating matters. I knew Christ would sustain me through the many layers of pain. I sought for clarity in my life and needed understanding about what life was truly about.

Just recently I had lunch with a woman, whose name I won't mention, and it changed my life. After sitting down to our lunch, I prayed, "Lord, help me to get something from this lady. What was that?" I thought to myself, "I'm a giver not a taker. I provide care for others. Did I just say that to God?"

I entered stark reality when she said, "Deb, I think I may have something for you. I read your book *Attitude Therapy* and found it helpful, but I do have something I feel you need that the Lord wants me to share with you."

She started sharing her testimony of pain and tragic sorrow. She recounted numerous times of sexual abuse by her religious father, who was an evangelist. She described the years of total terror, shame, resentment, anger, frustration, and how she just existed in life. Then she told me how she has suffered from numerous health problems and depression. She is a precious soul who had been taken to the very depths of hell by her earthly father. But, oh, how God loved her, reaching down, picking her up and dusting her off—calling her daughter, promising her joy.

His day is sacred to our Lord. Do not grieve, for the joy of the LORD is your strength. (Nehemiah 8:10 NIV)

My mouth fell wide open and didn't close one time. I even assisted with my hand. I remember wondering, "Does she see the expression on my face? How can I change it?"

I recall saying, "We have to go now."

With grace and poise she said, "I understand, dear."

The light from the window illuminated her face and literally danced around her head. I knew I had been with the Father as well. I was on sacred ground.

God had set my healing in motion some years ago. I remember being with Paul Young, author of *The Shack*, at a luncheon while folks asked him questions. I kept my protective outer covering on as he described in graphic detail his abuse—how the tribe would make a circle around him, even with his missionary parents within earshot, and rape him. I looked straight ahead chomping down on a carrot, holding it firmly between my teeth as my body went numb.

I had lost touch with reality to the point of waking up to Paul's voice calling, "Deb, Deb, Deb, hello—are you okay?"

"Yes," I smiled, making an excuse of lack of sleep the night before…and the night before that…and my entire life.

I know he knew at that moment, but I would not tip my hand or speak of it. I had a façade that was unshakable and it was "Stacy plastic" baby! Deb, and only Deb, would control this. I was not talking now or ever. How dare Paul Young talk and say such things? How could he say such things? Wasn't he raised properly? All of my father's words rang in my very soul. I was primed and controlled from a very early age, and I knew what to speak about (if anything). I grew up in the generation that was taught, "Children are to be seen and not heard." My father criticized anyone who spoke out about their parents.

My father had extramarital affairs. Everyone, including my mother, knew it and looked away. There was an air to his charm and personality that filled a room. No one could have won if they came up against him—yet in the end we are victorious in Christ.

In all things we are more than conquerors through Him who loved us. (Romans 8:37 NIV)

For everyone born of God overcomes the world. This is the victory that has overcome the world, even our faith. Who is it that overcomes the world? Only he who believes that Jesus is the Son of God. (1 John 5:4-5 NIV)

But thanks [be] to God, which giveth us the victory through our Lord Jesus Christ. (1 Corinthians 15:57)

I was brought up to act like a boy. I'm not joking; my father took me to the barber shop with him each week to have my hair cut short. I didn't wear a shirt until I was ten or eleven. I went everywhere dressed that way. In retrospect he encouraged me to act that way. He was very manipulative and I slept with him in place of my mother. As long as I can remember they didn't have a sexual relationship. When I think of a father abandoning their family, it's one thing, but when I recall how often he left us and then came back home, it was an emotional rollercoaster. He's here—he's not. Honestly, I'm not sure how or why, but my mother allowed me to sleep with him. I certainly don't remember jumping up and down excitedly chanting, "Pick me, pick me," rather it was understood.

My father self-soothed a lot and always fidgeted with my hair or rubbed my shoulder in one spot. I hated when he would obsessively do this. It just burned me to the very core of my soul. I recall lying on his lap in church, knowing what he was doing and how he touched me was wrong, yet somehow it was connected to a much bigger picture.

Sunday's always bothered me. It seemed everyone napped except for me. I hated going to bed. Until just recently, I have been anxious for years before going to bed, and really haven't slept soundly for a long time. All through the night I am constantly watching the door out of fear. I remember acting as though I was sleeping when he came to bed. As I'm writing this, I feel myself starting to shut down emotionally. I feel on one hand I am allowing myself to be comforted, yet on the other hand I nearly hate myself for saying anything about him. There are those who knew him that would be shocked to hear of his behavior towards his daughter, or would they?

In less than twenty-four hours after God delivered me, I went "fishing." I needed to hear from those who knew him. What did they know? How did he affect them? Were there other victims? Then the phone call came and I was sickened. I had asked for it and wanted to know, but I wasn't sure if I was ready to hear a story of how my father had attempted to punish another young family member with his tormented sexual desires. Upon the admission, I was shocked and a frantic trembling mess. How could I be crying and throwing up? My sweet husband ran to me, holding my hair out of my face and lovingly patted my forehead dry with a towel. My anger and the sheer weakness in my knees were very confusing to me. I had to see someone and it had to be now.

I walked into the counselor's office, nervous, timid, and very fearful. I felt like a small crouching animal with all of life's burdens strapped on my shoulders. As we walked through the hallway to her office, it felt like an eternity. I just wanted to run as I had my whole life from this awful pain inside. Sitting down we started to chat and I felt as though my head was spinning. I took a deep breath, choosing a spot on the wall I began my journey. I didn't take my eyes off of that spot—it was as if a movie was playing as I focused on recounting the days, minutes, and seconds of my journey called "Life."

I remember thinking, "Perhaps if I don't make eye contact she won't believe me." I quickly dismissed that thought because I didn't believe me either. I had been groomed my whole life to believe it wasn't right to say the things I was saying. When my father would hear others expressing their life stories, he would literally become outraged that a child would say such things about their parents. My last memories were of him being in the hospital with me helping him the way I always did.

I was assisting by helping them put him on the MRI table when he said, "My daughter is writing a book. It will probably come out before I die. You would think she would wait until I was gone to talk badly about me."

They laughed and laughed, but I felt once again like the odd man out. I wondered how in all of his pain and conflict he could still be flirting...in front of me.

Afterwards he brought it up again by saying, "Well, Deb, if I am alive they'll think what daughter would do that—whereas if I'm dead they'll say at least she waited until he was dead to talk poorly about him!"

Talk about controlling from the grave! I found in my prayer journal the entire conversation and the prayers I prayed over him that day. As I replay the story in my mind, I remember admitting he had abandoned us and how difficult life had been in my first book. I really and truly thought that was what he meant.

On his death bed he kept saying, "I'm sorry, I'm sorry," repeatedly to me as I wiped his brow and changed his diaper.

I said, "For what?"

He said, "You know."

That's as far as it got. I was afraid of what he would say next, but he was never able to go there.

Janice: WOW! What a story and the way you continued to help him even after all those years of abuse. I don't know if I would have been able to do the same. Because of abuse, I think maybe the love we feel for our parents is buried somewhere deep inside until circumstances present themselves, then our love and concern for them surfaces. Deb, I think in spite of the abuse you experienced there was a part of you that always hoped for your dad to change. I know you must have made a difference for him in the end by allowing the Lord to love him through you—giving you the courageous ability to give to a man who had taken so much.

Deb: When I reflect on all the years when my heart was broken, my dreams shattered, my relationships strained, and my struggle with sin, I know it was the Lord who carried me. It was His footprints in the sand, and they couldn't have been any more significant than they are right now.

You know, Janice, we are made up of memories, whether good or bad. These memories have molded and shaped us into the people we are. The broken road has given us directions not explicit enough to guide us through without scars, yet I feel that in my sin, shame, and brokenness He was the One who carried me. I wish I hadn't wasted so much time and had stopped earlier when I heard Him calling.

The light is what I have been receiving. The sunshine of my life (God) has illuminated the dark hiding places of my soul. His light, which is His Truth, is changing me, I am tearing down all the walls I have erected through my brokenness, and He is bringing the much needed healing I have been seeking.

For the word of God is living and active. Sharper than any double-edged sword, it penetrates even to dividing soul and spirit, joints and marrow; it judges the thoughts and attitudes of the heart. (Hebrews 4:12 NIV)

I don't want to control my thoughts any longer. I want to be a puppet on a string for God—Him working in me, for me, and controlling my every movement, my every thought, and using my gifts for the building up of His Kingdom. I realize though that it will be through my emotional healing that all the limitations will be lifted to enable Him to lead and guide me where He wants me to go. "Use me Lord," I cry out from the depths of my soul. The day I was born, He wrote His instructions upon my heart. However, years of hurt have kept me from knowing those instructions, but His light now shines brightly within me revealing the secrets of my heart. No more hiding! My shame is revealed and true freedom has begun.

"This is the covenant I will make with the house of Israel after that time," declares the LORD. "I will put my law in their minds and write it on their hearts. I will be their God, and they will be my people." (Jeremiah 31:33 NIV)

Chapter 4

The Element of Fear

For God hath not given us the spirit of fear; but of power, and of love, and of a sound mind. (2 Timothy 1:7)

Janice: From our earliest moments fear is determined to control us. Its ultimate desire is to place limitations around us so we won't reach our potential in God. Satan's plan to instill fear rapes us of our talents and gifts before we have the chance to use them. Being stripped of all spiritual soundness, fear produces cowardice and timidity in which we are afraid to be who we really are. Instead of speaking with boldness we shrink back, hiding in the shadows. But God's plan is one of divine mercy in which we have the power and resources in His name to thwart every attempt the enemy uses to destroy us through fear.

I believe fear comes as a result of generational curses. I inherited this evil through my family line. At the young age of four I became aware of its all encompassing power. Fear riddled my thoughts continually as I was afraid my mother would drown me, especially when she washed my hair at the kitchen sink. For reasons unknown, I always thought she wanted to harm me. I suppose the resentment and anger she felt towards my father was just so close to the surface that she wanted to hurt him any way she could. Maybe the thought of killing his children was running around in her mind, and I intuitively picked up on them. I can't say for sure that was the reason, but I had strong feelings she might hurt me.

You see, my father was physically abusive and felt he needed to control her every move. She lived very isolated and was instructed by him to never open the door for anyone unless he was home, that included family members. She lived with the drapes closed every day until he returned from work. At some point she was brave enough to leave him, but again was drawn back into his web of deceit with his pleas that he would do better. Much to her dismay, on the way home he beat her for leaving him in the first place.

My daily life consisted of fights occurring between my parents: my dad beat my mother, mother threatened suicide. Vivid memories fill my mind of those chilling words that she would scream after another physical encounter, "I'll kill myself!" She stood in his face, taunting him, "I'll show you!" She was in control of her own destiny, even if that meant ending her life. Like a broken record, I played those words over and over in my mind. It's no surprise I suffered from nightmares, too, my dreams narrating the internal war raging inside of me. Every night I awoke in terror, dreaming of snakes crawling all over me. I could actually feel her pain. Her life was out of control and void of all hope. After her death, the dreams stopped.

Have you ever experienced paralyzing fear? I'm talking about fear that's so real you can almost touch it? It's the kind of fear that stops you dead in your tracks. Fear so powerful you're afraid to even breathe when you awaken in the middle of the night after a bad dream. Well, I have. I lived this way with my parents. I didn't know from one day to the next what would happen. I only knew I was afraid. I constantly feared something bad happening to me or someone in my family, and eventually it did. I guess I just thought the way I lived was normal. Unfortunately, that's what happens to people who live with abuse, they start to think of it as being normal.

Victim of Bullying

Janice: Most of my childhood memories aren't pleasant ones. I clearly remember trying to be inconspicuous so no one would notice me. Being seen only meant the ugliness I felt would be magnified even more, so I used school to escape the humiliation. In spite of my circumstances, I was a good student and excelled in sports, staying active so I didn't have time to think about the words that hurt me. If you've ever been the object of name calling and insults, you know just how bad you start to feel about yourself. I can't even bring myself to repeat all the names I was called because they are just too ugly to mention. My physical attributes were often the target, which usually started with making fun of my feet, my lips, my backside, and basically every feature of my body. Naturally I became overly self-conscious about my appearance, believing I was defective and worthless. I couldn't see anything good about me.

Everyone seemed to be in on the action when it came to tearing me apart piece by piece. Even the adults who were guardians seemed to enjoy what was happening to me. I was a human punching bag for anyone to take out their frustration. I didn't have one friend or one adult I could trust to defend or protect me. Truly I was alone and it was open season. Being bullied only added to the distress of being abandoned by my family. My self-esteem and confidence level was at an all time low, and it looked as if there was little hope for me.

You may be asking, "How is it that a child so young can feel that kind of deep loss?" I would say to you, "That even a child has hopes and dreams." Just because children are small and immature doesn't mean they don't care about life or the direction they're headed. I personally felt my life was over before it even began because of the problems thrown at me so early. Everything in my life pointed to failure. Even the areas of my life in which I did excel were ridiculed, tearing apart any confidence I may have had regarding my abilities. I was so beaten down I was barely able to pull myself up emotionally. Little by little my emotional strength left until I was unable to help myself anymore, and I eventually gave into defeat.

Although I was unable to see it at the time, God had a plan to bring me to a place of freedom. He can do the same for any of us, we just have to ask. We must be willing to dig in and hang on. What it will take to deliver us is so worth the ride.

Deb: Oh my dear Janice, I hurt for you. I hear that sweet and tender child within you. She is still alive, and in the name of Jesus Christ, I thank Him right this moment for her. I thank Him for your life, and I ask Him to touch you in a mighty way. I feel the unsteadiness, lack of confidence, and the pain associated with coming up the way you did. I ask my Redeemer to heal you—as He is with the very writing of this book. I, too, was bullied, but I fought back. As a matter of fact I fought back when there was no bullying at all. I fought back if I walked into a room of puppies! I was hyper-sensitive and hyper-vigilant as long as I can remember.

Janice: Deb, I fought back but the bullying was so intimidating I backed down in hurt and defeat. To this day I have a strong inclination against injustice, and I get very angry when I see others taking advantage of weaker individuals. It wasn't so much that I was a weak person, but the continual name calling eventually wore me down to the point I just felt I couldn't fight back anymore. Intimidation and fear are tools often used by insecure people to subdue another person into submission or retreat. It is far more common than we can imagine in our schools and society as a whole. Unfortunately, it is often dismissed by school officials and guardians because no one wants to get involved. We often hear or know of students who are bullied almost every day and endure a list of insulting behaviors from their peers.

A few years ago a story in the news told about a fifteen-year-old girl being bullied by two different groups of teenagers. After months of abuse she gave into the pressure and took her own life. Pictures splashed across the TV screen showing a group of students beating down another student and causing severe injury while adults stood by refusing to get involved. It is also common among families to hear of a child being bullied by a parent or maybe even both parents. This to me is the worst kind of bullying because the child has no protection and no place of security. There is nowhere to run and no one to run to. The one person he or she is suppose to trust the most is the one tearing them down and abusing them. I found myself in this kind of situation, too. Those who were guardians over me mistreated me, and didn't seem to mind when others did the same. If by some chance you are the one who is the bully, chances are that you too were a victim of someone else's abuse. You can stop abusing right now by making the choice to ask Jesus Christ to come into your life and change you.

Deb: Have you ever noticed how bullies are experts in using fear and intimidation? They seem to know which buttons to push to get a reaction. Maybe the reason they're so good at what they do is because at some point in their lives they too were the victim of someone else's abuse. They learned to disparage another in an attempt to bring them down to their level of inadequacy because they themselves lacked self-confidence. Somehow they get a feeling of superiority by demeaning someone else. In a sick way they feel in control.

Janice: Like many children of abuse, I was especially fearful and distrusting because of the wounds of hurt inflicted on me, so I developed a mistrust of everyone. It didn't matter if they were the nicest person in the world, all I could see was fear of anyone getting close to me. The ugly names left lasting scars on my heart that have taken me years to recover from. Though the pain of those hurtful words no longer has the same affect on me, I still have moments of insecurity and doubt about myself. But I continue striving to overcome by not allowing insecurity to determine my outlook on life.

Deb: My youngest son was a victim of bullying in the school he attended. Ultimately a broken bone in his hand was the result of this behavior during a gym class and required immediate surgery. Having Christ in my heart, I didn't want to raise a "stink" about it so I simply scheduled surgery, and got my son professional counseling to help him in disarming these bullies. It wasn't until I walked into the school to sign my daughter out for an appointment that a teacher, who must have had the kind of background in abuse you mentioned, walked over to my son who had just had surgery, and postured himself over him while he was sitting down. He told him that the bullying had not occurred on his watch. I lost it! I ran interference for my son and swiftly stood between the two of them, and promptly told the teacher to not use his dominating and powerful position to intimidate my son. I was outraged to the point of physically acting out, but the Holy Spirit intervened and I calmed down. I'll never forget the look on my son's face as he saw that I had witnessed a small part of what he put up with all year.

Janice: Deb, you absolutely did the right thing in stepping between your son and that teacher. We all must realize our responsibility to protect our children from abuse of any kind. Words have power to uplift and encourage, or bring us down no matter who utters them. Our children are the most vulnerable ones in our society, with the tendency to believe whatever we tell them. As parents, we must be acutely aware of the way we speak to our children, and how we allow others to speak to them. Parental authority wields a lot of power and must be handled with the utmost care and concern. Unfortunately, not all parents love their children. Some even inflict deep, lasting wounds that leave their child in an emotional heap. A parent who says to his child, "You're stupid," strips him of dignity and self-worth. If left unchallenged, those few words of defeat take root, instilling fears and doubts about who they are and where they fit in life. From then on, their measuring rod of self-worth will be the unloving words of an unmerciful and unkind parent or adult.

Deb: Janice, I too suffered abuse verbally, physically, and emotionally. God has me in a beautiful place of healing. I must admit it wasn't always that way, instead I was always "fighting back" because I was always in hyper-alert mode, fearful and wounded. I loved my children desperately and clung too tightly to them. My hope was that they would be tough like me so that no one could ever hurt them. My expectations were far too much for them to handle because I had been in survival mode all of my life. With the hard fought battles I had won, I transferred my fears to my older children with the unnecessary determination to overcome and excel.

As you know, I have six children all of whom I love and adore. As I've aged, I've become mellower in my approach to them because His hand is upon me. However, having said that, I can assure you I'm not a perfect parent. As our "baggage" tries to get in the way, we need to remember the words of Jesus in John 8:32, one of my favorite scriptures, "And ye shall know the truth and the truth shall make us free." I am going through the process of recognizing this truth. I have always been hard on myself, even rigid at times in the expectations I have set. While I have developed a healthy self-esteem, I know my faults and where I don't measure up to His Word. I used to really care about pleasing everyone. Years ago He delivered and redeemed me to truly serve Him, first by teaching me to put His will above my own, my husband, and my children. Once I learned this lesson, it has been easier to not measure myself by the standards of other people or my own unrealistic standards. When you are pleasing to Him you are generally pleasing to others.

The Power of Fear

Janice: Webster's dictionary defines fear as "being afraid of; or expecting with alarm."[5] The acronym I like to use is **False Evidence**

Appearing **R**eal. Fear is the appearance of something that doesn't physically exist. It's an illusion, not a reality. Imaginations are "the act or power of forming a mental image of something not present to the senses or never before wholly perceived in reality"[6] according to The Dake Annotated Reference Bible. A lie is first conveyed through our imaginations or minds, the vehicle Satan uses to plant lies, doubts, and anything else he desires to use to bring about our ruin. He studies us from every angle, devising plans and points of attack, waiting for the perfect moment to bring total devastation to our lives. Most of us aren't even aware our imaginations play such a vital role in what we say and do. Satan is counting on our ignorance.

Scripture tells us, "Be sober, be vigilant; because your adversary the devil walks about as a roaring lion, seeking whom he may devour" (1 Peter 5:8). As long as we remain ignorant of his devices, he works unseen, wreaking havoc and chaos intended to waste us. "Casting down imaginations, and every high thing that exalts itself against the knowledge of God, and bringing into captivity every thought to the obedience of Christ." (2 Corinthians 10:5). The *Dake Annotated Reference Bible* says, "We are to demolish all theories, reasonings and any high system of ethics, religion, mythology, metaphysics, sublime doctrines, or philosophy set forth to defy the knowledge of God."[7]

In my own failure to bring my thoughts under control of the Holy Spirit, I opened the door for Satan to bring me under slavery and bondage. I didn't knowingly open the door, but my behavior laid the groundwork for me to be bound to a life of discouragement and defeat. The Dake Bible states, "We are to take every thought prisoner and lead it into captivity to obey Christ. Lascivious, vain and evil thoughts of all kinds are brought down and made obedient to His laws. That includes any thinking contrary to virtue, purity and righteousness."[8] When we yield our minds to thoughts contrary to God's Word, we can easily be taken captive to do Satan's bidding, meaning he can put whatever thoughts into our imaginations at will, and we'll obey them.

Deb: Satan is acutely skilled in using our imaginations against us, pulling us from faith into fear by mere suggestion or thought. We form mental images based on what others have said about us or by any suggestive image that enters our minds, then we act on what we see, think, or feel. Giving heed to discouraging words gives them power over us instead of God empowering us through His Word. "The mind is a battlefield"[9] to quote Joyce Meyer, and we must deal a death blow to anything contrary to truth.

Coping with Fear

Janice: Fear is debilitating and powerful enough to induce emotional and physical paralysis. It has the uncanny ability to keep us from achieving success in our work, our marriages, or any of our relationships. The power of its force leaves us feeling helplessness and lost. We feel trapped by a situation that appears to have no way out of it. Then the pity party starts, we reason nothing good ever happens to us, and we give up without a fight. This is Satan's ploy—to get us to give in and give up. Another person however, may respond in a totally different way by acting out rebelliously. They may say something to the effect of, "How dare you say I can't do this! I live my own life as I choose. No one tells me what I can and cannot do." The word *failure* compels them to prove everyone wrong, especially those who wish to see them fail. Both are walking in fear even though their responses are quite different.

Loss and trauma produces oppression if left unchecked. The enemy cunningly looks for our weakest link; using every opportunity he can find to oppress us. If we continue to let fear stay active in us, we will remain emotionally weak, hindering our own emotional and spiritual development. We're pushed out of God's plan for our lives and into the corner of defeat. That's why the love and support of family and friends is so important. Unconditional love and support gives us strength, calming the emotional storms raging inside of us. Failure to receive unconditional love and support, as well as the influence of circumstances and events, may deepen the emotional abyss we find ourselves falling into. Our only hope is through a relationship with Jesus Christ.

Deb: Our potential must first be grounded in our walk of faith by accepting who God says we are. Achieving success in business, family, or anything we endeavor to do must come first through trusting Christ. Many times we define who we are by self-imposed ideas or ideas someone else has burdened us with, and ultimately we come away disappointed because our hope was in the wrong thing.

Janice: Deb, life is more than the material things that surround us or the things we hope to achieve in this life. First and foremost our aim in life should not be to live selfishly, but rather to give ourselves away, and love as Christ would love. My dear friend, love is what will change the world. When we put off this body we will stand before our Creator, and He won't see us because of our achievements or our material wealth. No! He'll see us through His Son Jesus Christ or through His archenemy Satan. The question will be, "Who did we live our lives for?"

Our desire above all should be to achieve success in our relationships with others and our relationship with our heavenly Father. We all have a desire for spiritual wholeness in spirit, mind, and body. When we put God first in our lives, all the things we desire can be ours if we believe.

But seek ye first the kingdom of God, and his righteousness;
and all of these things shall be added unto you. (Matthew 6:33)

Deb: The more we chat, the more I realize we have more in common than we had originally thought. For years, fear and intimidation were the two constants in my life. I was a very fearful child. From my earliest memories my father was very strict, as well as verbally and physically abusive. I would be so afraid, I would pee in my pants. I lived in fear for so long that it became a way of life for me. I think the adrenaline was always pumping because I was constantly running from one event to another event! As I continued my walk through life, I made myself busy. I involved myself and the kids in everything—sports, music, church, you name it. I grew a business from one employee (me) to 4,000 employees in seven states. I was involved on boards, owned a consulting service, and traveled nationally for speaking engagements. Every time the Lord helped me to slow down, I sped back up. I was running straight out from fear.

I like to claim the following scripture: "Fear thou not for I am with thee; be not dismayed; for I am thy God: I will strengthen thee: yea, I will help thee; yea I will uphold thee with the right hand of my righteousness" (Isaiah 41:10). With that being said, my fear of even speaking about fear is less than it used to be. Fear is like a cancer of the soul. If we are fearful then Christ can't shine through us. We can't help anyone when we are incapacitated. He is the Great Physician of our souls, and we must cry out to Him to help us. Jesus asks us, "Why are ye fearful, O ye of little faith?" (Matthew 8:26). Then He will rebuke the winds and the seas and there be a great calm. I don't know about you, Janice, but I can tell you He has worked in my life many times. He, and only He, has calmed the winds and brought about the calm in my soul. So I stand on His promises knowing without a doubt that His word and His promises can be trusted.

Janice: Fear had free reign in my life for a long time. Like you, Deb, it was a cancer of the soul that took over much of my life. My mother's suicide, coupled with being abandoned by my father, reinforced every fear I had. I feared rejection, abandonment, death, authority, success, and failure all at the same time. How can that be? It's amazing how its all encompassing power took total control over my life. But God, in His amazing grace, gave me a way of escape through His life giving Word. Scripture says it so beautifully; "For God hath not given us the spirit of fear; but of power, and of love, and of a sound mind" (2 Timothy 1:7).

God's desire is perfection in our spirit, mind, and body. He doesn't want fear to rule us, but the weight of sin has crushed us, driving many of us to look for love in all the wrong places. The bars are full of people aching to be loved. They sit at the bar night after night hoping to meet that one special person who is the answer to their deepest need. My friend, I've met that special person, His name is Jesus Christ. He's saying to us all, "Come to Me, I want to give you the riches that are mine, I want to give you my heart. I have the love you've been searching for your whole life." God's uncon-ditional love is where true spiritual and emotional freedom is found, not in the empty vain love the world offers.

The world's definition of love is constantly changing, making it impossible to trust. God never changes. He's the same yesterday, today, and tomorrow. Like me, some of you have spent your entire life searching for this kind of love and may be asking, "Is it possible to experience such unconditional love?" Absolutely! The question to be answered though is, "How do we tap into the power that fuels it?" The answer is very simple, "We put on Christ." First, we recognize our need to be rescued by Him. Secondly, we accept Him as our Savior, and thirdly we study the Word to be molded and shaped into His image. Only then is His character revealed through us to others. God has made a way of escape from fear and that is through the power of His love. ***Beautiful!***

Deb: You are right about the scriptures, my sweet sister. For years I dutifully studied the scriptures because it was on my "To Do List." I approached God in a robotic, self-organized, and self-righteous way, doing my "duty" in the name of Jesus. Several years ago it became apparent to me that I didn't truly trust and believe God like I said I did. In all my seeking I was still fearful in the closest of relationships, including my relationship with Him. I got honest about putting limitations on my relationship with God, and that being a "dutiful" daughter of Christ was not good enough. I realized that my mechanical approach to God was not producing the fruit that I so longed for and needed to bear. I can honestly tell you though that "things got better when I got better."

I decided to pray for a closer walk with the Lord so that I could learn trust and obedience, while casting my cares upon Him, and believing His will to be accomplished in my life. The desire to draw closer to Him was there, but I needed His help to trust Him in all areas of my life, as well as build a **real** and lasting relationship with

Him. Instead of praying about the problems I saw in others, I told Him how I longed to have faith the size of a mustard seed. I asked Him to do an authentic work within me that would teach me to trust and believe Him. As we know, living our lives in fear and distrust has produced paralysis that takes over everything we attempt to do. Drawing closer to God and letting go of fear is difficult, but altogether possible when the One who loves and understands us is by our side, pulling us deeper and deeper into a relationship with Him.

The Lies We Believe

Janice: Satan doesn't have the legal right to come into our lives without permission. Some situation or event must first occur for him to have the legal right to enter. If you were going to someone's house for a visit, the only way you would have access to enter would be either by invitation or your possession of a key to the door. Likewise, the quickest and fastest way for Satan to gain access into our lives is either through invitation or having in his possession a key to the front door of our lives. So what might that key be? It could be an area of deception in which we believe something false, embracing a lie of some kind, or an area of sin in which we refuse to confront. The *Merriam-Webster Dictionary* definition of a lie is "a deliberate action of making a false statement or an intentional untruth."[10] Every word uttered by Satan is a lie because there is not one ounce of truth in him. He is the father of lies and has spent eons honing his skills in the art of lying. For those of us who are already founded in Christ, it should come as no surprise this is the way in which he operates.

In whom the god of this world hath blinded the minds of them which believe not, lest the light of the glorious gospel of Christ, who is the image of God, should shine unto them.
(2 Corinthians 4:4)

Make no mistake, Satan is the god of this world, and his objective is to blind us in our discernment. Once blinded, our minds become darkened, and we eagerly accept anything masquerading as truth. Without a strong defense, he cunningly establishes whatever trick of deception he chooses, planting it into our minds. Believe me he knows our weaknesses, and preys on them hoping to catch us unaware. The *Discovery Channel* airs programs on television frequently about animals that prey on weaker and more vulnerable animals. The hunter always looks for the weakest one in the group, and then sets his sights to kill or maim them. This is the same exact way Satan works on us. He looks for a weak spot in our nature. Once he has discovered our weakness, we then become his victim or prey. Be very careful, my friend, in what you hear and what you believe because it may be the one thing that destroys your life.

Deb: Janice, when I pray I rebuke Satan in the name of Jesus Christ. I claim the precious blood and mercy of our God. Scripture says, "You, dear children, are from God and have overcome them, because the one who is in you is greater than the one who is in the world" (1 John 4:4 NIV). I will only serve one Master, our Almighty God. The reason I pray this way is to be certain that I crowd Satan out daily as I know he is steadily pursuing me. I've told you before, and I will say it until the day I die, "Jesus is the same yesterday, today, and forever." We are living in modern-day Bible stories. I never want to say I'm shocked at anything because as we read the Word of God, it's all been done before. King Solomon spoke with such wisdom when he said, "The thing that hath been, it [is that] which shall be; and that which is done [is] that which shall be done: and [there is] no new [thing] under the sun" (Ecclesiastes 1:9). If we truly desire to live in the spiritual realm, we need to get out of the carnal realm.

The Trying of Our Faith

Janice: Deb, I certainly agree with all you've said. We do live in modern times, yet we continue to struggle with the same problems and temptations as generations before us. More and more I realize how we mere humans are really all the same. We all come from different walks of life, yet our struggles are similar. I want to elaborate for a minute on the role temptations play in our lives, and how they help to strengthen us spiritually. Temptation is commonly associated with sinful, forbidden desires. I dare say most are unaware of its enticement because it presents itself as something beautiful and desirable. Satan isn't going to offer us anything horned and ugly, it will be beautiful, enticing us with desires hidden within our hearts.

That's why it's especially important to make sure our desires line up with God's desires. It's not the mere suggestion or idea of temptation that gets us in trouble, but it's the giving in and lingering on those thoughts.

God's Word tells us, "There hath no temptation taken you but such as is common to man: but God [is] faithful, who will not suffer you to be tempted above that ye are able; but will with the temptation also make a way to escape, that ye may be able to bear [it]" (1 Corinthians 10:13). Some believe God tempts us to sin, but His Holy Word tells us that our own lust is what pulls us away. "But every man is tempted, when he is drawn away of his own lust, and enticed" (James 1:14). The term "drawn away" simply means to be lured away or tempted by unwholesome desires. Even the most godly and holy among us are tempted at some point in our Christian walk.

Jesus, who was perfect and without sin, was also tempted by Satan when He fasted forty days in the wilderness, "Then was Jesus led up of the Spirit into the wilderness to be tempted of the devil" (Matthew 4:1). The wilderness represents a dry solitary place, a place of testing and trial. It's a place for the purpose of revealing our character. So why does God allow us to go through trying times? "Knowing [this], that the trying of your faith worketh patience. But let patience have [her] perfect work, that ye may be perfect and entire, wanting nothing" (James 1:3-4). God's desire for us is that we be perfect in our faith and trust towards Him so that we lack nothing. Faith says, "God, I trust You though I can't see what's ahead of me." Genuine faith opens the door for God's total provision, whether that provision is physical, emotional, or spiritual. When faith is real there is complete confidence in God's ability, there's peace despite circumstances, and then there is a joy that comes from inward abiding peace.

Abiding means we are to be constant and steady in our faith. If our faith is impure there will be doubt and unbelief, incomplete actions, and swerving or instability in our actions. This is not pleasing to God, for anyone who wants to please God must come in faith believing that He is who He says He is. You may question, "Why do I need endurance?" God's ultimate desire is for us to be perfect without spot, blemish, or defects. We need endurance to build our patience which increases our ability to withstand hardships or adversity. "And not only [so], but we glory in tribulations also: knowing that tribulation worketh patience" (Romans 5:3). This means waiting upon the Lord to move during His own times and seasons. He isn't bound by time, but we are and this is why patience is so important to our faith walk. We learn trust through our suffering. "Though he were a Son, yet learned he obedience by the things which he suffered" (Hebrews 5:8).

Many times trials are so painful we wonder will we ever make it through. We need times of testing because they prove our faith to be genuine, or prove our lack of commitment to God. If our faith is proven to be true, then God can entrust us with His most Holy Word. If we are found to be lacking, then we can expect another round of trials up ahead. So, my friend, what does temptation reveal about your character?

Chapter 5

Rejection and Self-Rejection

But first he must suffer many things and be rejected by this generation. (Luke 17:25 NIV)

Rejection is the action of refusing to accept or love another person or thing. None of us like how rejection makes us feel, but it's inevitable that each of us will experience it at some point in our lives. Whether it is through our career, from our peers, or through a relationship, we all will eventually come face-to-face with it. Jesus Christ, though He was God, was no different than us in that He, too, suffered rejection by His own generation. Their denial of His Godhood undoubtedly broke His heart as it would anyone because everything He did was out of love for us. However, His ability to resist their rejection came from His relationship with His Heavenly Father. He was so rooted and grounded in the love of His Father, that rejections impact couldn't stop Him from completing His mission. He kept His eyes on the prize of salvation for each of us. This is what set Him apart from us. His focus was on redeeming God's people and not to win a popularity contest. Our mission should be to become more like Christ every day. It is with certainty that we are going to be rejected at some point, but it doesn't have to destroy us.

No Respecter of Persons

Janice: Rejection has a way of creeping into our lives and taking from each of us. Being no respecter of persons, its gnarly fingers reach the greatest to the least of us. We may all look and act differently, with some lives more rewarding and fuller than others, yet it finds a way to touch each of us. No matter which part of the world we come from or our station in life, we can count on it finding us. The way we handle rejection determines our outcome. Some argue and fight over small insignificant matters, creating situations that reinforce the rejection they feel. Some put on a persona of perfection to hide their true feelings, pretending to be something they are not, while others demonstrate a haughty spirit in which they believe they are somehow superior to others. Then there are those who wallow in self-pity and really don't want to change. Our pride whispers we are the only one who feels this way, reinforcing the notion we are alone. Loneliness then isolates us from getting help for ourselves and the cycle repeats itself.

For those who appear to have it all together, upon closer inspection we see the damaging effects low self-esteem and rejection have had on their emotions. It is demonstrated in our endless pursuit for perfection. Perfection says, "If only I could do everything perfectly, if only I had the perfect body or the right career then I'd be accepted." We presume reaching perfection is the cure all to our problems, so we work tirelessly to attain it. In the end though, we find emptiness where no real joy or satisfaction is ever realized. Why do we continue to pursue things that disappointment us? I think we have this haunting voice in the back of our minds that says, "We're never going to be good enough." So we continue the endless cycle of trying to be perfect, yet our pursuit for perfection will never end this side of heaven. Perfectionism creates in us an unhealthy desire to control our surroundings and the people in our lives. This, of course, ruins our relationships because the situations we try to avoid inevitably come up again and again. This only fuels our obsession to control every situation all the more.

Manipulation and control are sins akin to sorcery. We do everything in our power to gain control over others so we twist them to behave in a way that makes us feel safe. No one wants to talk about the sinfulness of controlling others because we live in a society where it's common for women to control their husbands using sex, control their children by withholding love and acceptance, and meticulously controlling our surroundings by demanding that everyone live up to an unrealistic standard we have set for ourselves. It's an attitude of, "Do exactly as I say or else!" Or else I withhold my affection, or pout until I get my way, or argue and fight my point until I have completely worn down my opponent so they give into my demands.

Men are just as guilty of the same types of behaviors as women, but I think some women's behaviors are far worse because they want the power to control. Their desire is to be in the driver's seat of their marriage and family, usurping the husband's authority given to him by God as the spiritual head of the home. We live in a society in which women are encouraged to be the driving force in their families, but in God's eyes this is disorder. God has an order that brings safety to the family, but when disorder becomes the "order of the day," confusion is at its core. "For where envying and strife [is], there [is] confusion and every evil work" (James 3:16). The driving force behind our striving behavior is rooted in fear. We're afraid of losing control, and we can't fathom someone else leading us. We want to lead ourselves.

There's another reason we feel we must control everyone around us. We are afraid others will see us as we are. We're afraid of allowing others to see us with our numerous flaws and weaknesses. Oh my! We can't allow that to happen! So we spend hours working on our outward appearance, not realizing we need to fix what's inside. We wash and curl our hair, paint our nails, prepare our make-up, and spend an hour or longer choosing the right outfit to wear, hoping to hide who we really are.

"[Thou] blind Pharisee, cleanse first that [which is] within the cup and platter, that the outside of them may be clean also" (Matthew

23:26). In Jesus' day the spiritual leaders were guilty of being more concerned with their outward show than with the interior motives of their hearts. We can make our outward appearance stunning and beautiful, but that will not change the ugliness of sin in our hearts. My friend, our outward appearance will not matter if our hearts are full of sin.

Let it not be that outward [adorning] of plaiting the hair, and of wearing of gold, or of putting on of apparel; But [let it be] the hidden man of the heart, in that which is not corruptible, [even the ornament] of a meek and quiet spirit, which is in the sight of God of great price. (1 Peter 3:3-4)

God is after our hearts, not how we look outwardly. His desire is that we be meek (humble) and quiet (calm) which draws His attention to us. In so doing, we find favor in His eyes. I know we've all heard the saying; "Beauty is only skin deep but ugly is to the bone." There's a lot of truth in that saying. Let us with boldness be who God originally designed us to be. You are beautiful the way you are so stop being plastic, it comes across as mindless and unfeeling. Let go of the self-doubt and insecurity that make us go to great lengths to hide ourselves, and openly declare with joy that we are made in the image and likeness of our great God. Let's take on His attitude of love and acceptance of others, but also acceptance of ourselves. This should be the image we want others to see.

Deb: You know I find that I have an armadillo defense mechanism that comes up when people approach me about certain things.

It has taken me years to discern the protective outer covering that almost physically comes up within me. I have found that mine is generally hidden behind such words as, "I am fine," "That isn't bothering me," or "No, I wasn't hurt." My fakeness, if you will, generally comes up as dishonest feelings in a relationship. It has taken our Lord and Savior years to show me the root of this behavior within me. All the while I might have been saying something about another person who acted fake or had a plastic voice. WOW! Sin is sin; whether we are aware it is going on within us or not.

For years I wrestled with who was in control—me or the Great I Am. There is a clue there, but I am a slow learner. Is it the Master of the universe or me who is trying to manage my stuff and everyone else I come into in contact with? I had great excuses. My mother became ill when I was in my teens. She suffered long and hard and I was her primary care giver. I became a control freak in many ways, but this helped empower me even more. I had buried deep inside all the childhood sexual, physical, and emotional abuse. Now I believed the emergency was to keep her alive. I had one goal and one goal only because survival of the fittest had set in. In survival mode, I could've picked up a car with one hand had that been the problem. The adrenaline was rushing in and I was manic, afraid, and fighting with all I had. After she died, I continued fighting. I was in constant flight or fight mode. It's much like the soldiers who come home from battle and wrestle with Post Traumatic Stress disorder. I have wrestled with PTSD all my life. I tried in my teen years to snuff out my pain with the use of alcohol and drugs. I often lost my temper.

Even though I had given my life to Christ at an early age, He had massive amounts of work to do in me. I think those of us who have known extreme sadness and trauma are more aware of His need to straighten us out because everything is relevant. Those Christians who haven't known many seasons of pain, suffering, or problems are so settled in the everyday Christian life that they forget to grow. There isn't anything leaping out of their past inviting them to fully surrender. They are at status quo and nothing is pulling at them. I think this is a very dangerous place to be in our spirit, living in the status quo. We must seek Him with all of our hearts, daily, moment by moment in everything we do. You see, it's in the valley of our lives that God offers opportunity to grow our hearts in Him. It is growth season! Then we're on the mountain top and we feel His presence in every situation. We feel great joy when we can see Him working in our lives.

I wouldn't change anything because I know that He reached down and saved me. He protected me from the pain, confusion, and the total disappointment that my father, whom I trusted, would hurt me as a child. It is beyond anything my heart or mind can conceive! But on October 2, 2011, when my heart became totally His, I finally laid down my fears and need to control at His feet. I decided to get out of God's way allowing Him room to strengthen and grow me in Him. Suddenly, life became real and understandable to me. I stand amazed that I have been a Christian for over fifty years, and only recently have I allowed Him enough room to change me, and take away the pain and suffering. Total trust is the most awesome place to be in your relationship with Him. The day that my heart became totally His, without me holding on to one thing, is a day I will celebrate forever!

Janice: You're right! Sin is sin. My perfectionist tendencies came through a critical and judgmental spirit. I had in my mind that I had to be perfect physically and look a certain way. So when I met anyone I thought looked better than me, I was immediately threatened. Soon I began looking for ways to find fault with them. Somehow in my mind this sinful behavior elevated me, and made me feel somewhat better about myself. However, it was always short lived because I had set a standard that was unattainable. I simple felt I could never measure up to anyone or the expectations I had set for myself. I have discovered there will always be someone who looks better than me. None of us want to admit we are critical, but God's Word clearly tells us in Isaiah 58:9 that He will hear our prayers when we stop pointing the finger and stop speaking vanity. Conquering my critical tendencies hasn't been easy. It has been a deliberate seeking of God's ways that has changed me.

Deb: Oh, what rejoicing we experience within our souls when He delivers us, redeeming us from ourselves. "My grace is sufficient for you, for my power is made perfect in weakness" (2 Corinthians 12:9). Indeed our being perfect truly happens when we depend on

His grace and allow our inability to be perfected by the Master. I feel guilty when I think of our perfectionist ways of making our homes and our Thanksgiving tables perfect. I think women tend to control their environment to a fault, not relying on Jesus in every situation. I remember many times during the holidays, how I would put undue pressure on my kids while instructing them to set "the perfect table," missing out on the joy of their little hands and hearts helping me. I think of the years I stayed busy as a workaholic, pushing ahead so hard to "get it perfect," and missing out on His daily input. I was so focused on "perfection" I didn't invite Him in as often as I should have. Oh, my friend, you said it so beautifully when you said, "Deliberately seeking His will and His healing of us." Our purpose daily should be to always expose our hearts to Him for His approval and healing!

Janice: Perfection is a hard taskmaster, demanding way too much from us. Not only do we put extreme pressure on ourselves to perform, but we put the same unrealistic expectations on our families. Why do we subject ourselves to such grueling pursuits? Could it be we can't accept our failures or the failures of others? To me, failure meant weakness, and I couldn't possibly let anyone see me as incompetent. That would tear down the image I had erected, and would be way too painful to live through. "Thou shalt have no other gods before me" (Exodus 20:3). We are guilty of the sin of idolatry, worshipping the god of self and our own ideas when we demand everyone follow after us. I have been guilty of pushing my children to do things that caused resentment. It was my way or the highway because it was all about me. In an attempt to protect my precious ego, I have held my boys up, refusing to let them fail. In my mind their failure was a reflection on me and my ability to parent.

We keep our children from learning when we are constantly holding them up. Our own insecurities are the driving force behind our unrealistic expectations, and eventually the things we have demanded of others will blow up in our faces. There will be a breaking point. Either we will break down, or the ones we place unrealistic demands will break down. The truth, however painful it may be, is that we are broken individuals. As long as we put ourselves before God and others, we will continue down this destructive path and it will end in disappointment. "And he said unto me, my grace is sufficient for thee: for my strength is made perfect in weakness. Most gladly therefore will I rather glory in my infirmities, that the power of Christ may rest upon me" (2 Corinthians 12:9). I urge you today to let go for once and trust God. He does have all the answers, and your situation isn't too difficult for Him.

Suicide

Janice: November of 1967, my mother made good on her threats, fulfilling her own prophecy. She committed suicide in front of me and my siblings, leaving us to deal with the terrible events of that day. We had come home from a day of shopping, and even a five-year-old child can sense when something is amiss. Being overly sensitive to my mother's moods, I knew what she was about to do when I saw her holding the rifle. She beaconed for me to come to her, and I nervously approached her side. She sat on the edge of the bed holding the rifle, the butt sitting on the floor. Shaking with fear I begged her to reconsider. She spoke to me in hushed tones. I can't remember all she said, only, "I love you," and a kiss goodbye.

With blind determination, she walked into the living room and pointed the barrel of the rifle at her abdomen. Three of us children made a circle around her because we didn't know what else to do. My father saw her and walked over to take the rifle from her. The rifle was a hair-trigger gun; when barely touched it went off with a loud bang as she whirled around to get out of his reach. The force of the blast threw her to the floor. Screaming with terror, we didn't realize the full extent of what had just happened. The next few hours were spent talking to law enforcement officers trying to convince them of my dad's innocence.

Going to the funeral home was especially terrifying. I had never known anyone who had died and didn't know what to expect. Stepping through the entryway of the funeral home, my eyes darted nervously around the room. There she lay, motionless in a soft blue gown, her long dark hair pulled back revealing the beauty in her face. I didn't recall ever seeing her with such an untroubled expression. Deliberately tracing my finger across her cold skin, I stopped to touch her hand for the last time. My mother was gone! My baby sister reached for her, not realizing she would never feel the warmth of her arms again. Standing in silence, I stared at the face I loved, knowing this would be the last time. No matter the confusion or pain, she was my mother and I loved her and missed her immensely. The final chapter of her life had been written, and I would walk the rest of my life's journey without her.

According to Wikipedia, "Over one million people die by suicide every year. The World Health Organization (WHO) estimates that it is the thirteenth leading cause of death worldwide and the National Safety Council rates it sixth in the United States. It is a leading cause of death among teenagers and adults under 35. The rate of suicide is far higher in men than in women, with males worldwide three to four times more likely to kill themselves than females. There are an estimated 10 to 20 million non-fatal attempted suicides every year worldwide."[11] That's a huge number of people attempting to take their own lives any given day of the week. What drives a person to toy with the idea of taking their own life? My mother was emotionally spent trying to cope with the abuse and rejection my father dished out regularly. I believe this is what drove her over the edge. The day she died, she had every intention of paying him back, and suicide was the way she would do it.

Personally, I believe anger is one of the causes attributed to many suicide attempts. Suicidal thoughts are also attributed to moments of despair, vulnerability, and feelings related to hopelessness. Unfortunately many have killed themselves when they were having a bad day and nothing was going right. Maybe they made a horrible error and couldn't live with the consequences of their actions, or the pain they were experiencing at the moment was more than they could bear. In their minds the only way out was through death. "There hath no temptation taken you but such as is common to man: but God [is] faithful, who will not suffer you to be tempted above that ye are able; but will with the temptation also make a way to escape, that ye may be able to bear [it]" (1 Corinthians 10:13).

Emotions are capricious, affecting our moods and behavior from day to day and moment to moment. They are subject to rapid changes depending on the circumstances we find ourselves in at the time. That is what makes them so dangerous when they are out of control. **Never** rely on your emotions when making life altering decisions. That's why it's vitally important to bring them under the guidance of the Holy Spirit and not allow ourselves to be led by them. Suicide isn't a logical decision, but one based on wrong feelings and perceptions. If we knew all the facts before dramatically altering our lives forever, the decision to take our own life wouldn't even register on our radar.

The one question I often hear people ask is, "Why would someone want to take their own life?" Oh, how I have languished over hearing the news of someone I knew who had taken their life. It made no sense at all. They appeared to have so much going for them. I have grieved in my spirit over small children left behind because I am intimately aware of the pain and emptiness of losing a parent, especially in such a horrific way. Young children have little, if any understanding of the reasons behind their parent's death, and are unable to process what has happened to them. How could someone leave their small children behind and be unconcerned for their safety and well-being? I struggle to grasp understanding!

The most common response I've heard when asked why someone would do such a horrible thing is they were possibly depressed, angry, a victim of bullying, abused in every sense of the word, psychotic, emotionally unstable, and the list goes on. Some made the decision to end their lives out of vengeance. They were angry with another person, and wanted to make them pay for the pain they caused them. Hatred, jealousy, envy, bitterness, and unresolved anger pushed them to do the unthinkable. "Dearly beloved, avenge not yourselves, but [rather] give place unto wrath: for it is written, Vengeance [is] mine; I will repay, saith the Lord" (Romans 12:19).

If we look closer though, we see that these are just symptoms of a deeper issue within the heart. What are the real root causes of suicide? Frank and Ida Mae Hammond wrote a book titled, *Pigs in the Parlor*. In the book they have a chapter in which they place demonic spirits into groupings according to their behavior. The main root causes of suicide listed in their book are bitterness and depression. "Attached to bitterness are the thoughts and feelings of resentment, hatred, unforgiveness, violence, temper, anger, retaliation, murder, self-pity, loneliness, timidity, shyness, inadequacy, and ineptness. People suffering with depression battle feelings of despair, despondency, discouragement, defeatism, dejection, hopelessness, suicide, death, insomnia, and morbidity." [12]

Precious ones, God's desire is to deliver you once and for all from the pain that so deeply touches you. Your life is worth more than you could ever know. It truly grieves the heart of God to see you in such pain. That's why He came, so that He could understand and feel the things that affect us as humans. He wanted to identify with us. Please, I pray, heed what I am saying; if not for your own sake, then for the sake of your loved ones.

There's a country music song by Rascal Flatts called, "Why." One verse in the song says: "Oh, but I do have one burning question, who told you life wasn't worth the fight? They were wrong, they lied, now you're gone and we cry cause it's not like you to walk away in the middle of a song." My dear friend, there is nothing so horrible that it is worth ending your precious life. If you are contemplating suicide, there is a better way. You may be thinking your troubles will end when you take your last breath, but don't be deceived, your troubles are only beginning. Who you are when you die is who you are forever, so please seek help before making a wrong decision based on raw emotional pain. Suicide isn't the answer. Jesus is the only answer. Don't let one moment of utter despair take you down this road. In the end there will be nothing but regret and horror about the choice you have made. You are too valuable and too important to God to end your life so dramatically.

"When my father and my mother forsake me, then the Lord will take me up" (Psalm 27:10). Many of you have been forsaken by parents, friends, or even a spouse. My friend, you are not alone, the

Lord will stand with you and for you. I, too, was abandoned and left to my own devices after the death of my mother and the abandonment of my earthly father. But God in His grace (unmerited favor) and mercy became a father and a mother to me. This has given me great comfort throughout the years because I know He will never forsake me. His love is unconditional, letting me rest in the knowledge of His goodness. Leaning on Him, I find strength and joy to face whatever comes my way, for He is my source and the hope of my life. Nothing happens outside of Him that He isn't fully aware. He is intimately aware of all things pertaining to my life and your life, too. He is no respecter of persons, and loves each of us, even when we don't love Him back. We can count on people to fail us, but rest assured Christ never has and never will fail.

Rejection is cruel and hateful and must be torn down. It will eventually destroy us if left to grow unhindered, diminishing our chance of a genuine relationship with God. Why must we demolish this evil? Because inwardly we feel worthless, believing God could never love us the way we are. In our minds we reason if mom and dad can't love me, how is it possible that the God of the Universe could love me? The concept of unconditional love is just too hard to accept for the emotionally wounded. But, you see, that's the beauty of a loving God. He doesn't look on our faults and failures, but sees someone He laid down His life for on the cross at Calvary.

The enemy of our soul wants nothing more than to deprive us of a loving relationship with God. If we aren't careful to watch, his schemes will not only destroy us in this life, but in the life hereafter. "Be sober; be vigilant; because your adversary the devil, as a roaring lion, walks about seeking whom he may devour" (1 Peter 5:8). The word *sober* means to be temperate, serious, and reasonable. *Vigilant* means staying watchful and alert to danger or trouble. In other words, we are to be wide awake and watching for whatever ploy or tactics the enemy may use to gain entrance into our lives. Satan wants nothing more than to see us fail in our testimony. If he is successful in getting others to see us as hypocrites, our testimony to the world is blown. If Satan can defeat us through rejection, we are no longer a threat to his goals of silencing the truth of God's Word throughout the world. He will search for every opportunity to bring defeat as the tentacles of rejection reach into every facet of our lives. Know for certain you will face rejection, and it will likely come from someone you know. However, the way we conduct ourselves and deal with rejection is what determines our outcome.

The Humanity of Christ Jesus

He is despised and rejected of men; a man of sorrows and acquainted with grief: and we hid as it were our faces from him; he was despised and we esteemed him not. (Isaiah 53:3)

Jesus experienced rejection from those He knew and loved. They hid their faces, refusing to look at Him. How His heart must have broken into a million pieces. How He must have anguished knowing their secret thoughts. Although pained by their rejection, He knew

His true identity, and looked to the mission set before Him. His love was so great for us, He willingly chose to bear the cross, setting aside His own humanity that we might come to salvation. He simply refused to encumber Himself with worry about what people were saying. I can hear some of you saying, "Well, He was part God and part man; no wonder He was able to ignore the pain of rejection."

And God said; "Let us make man in our image, after our likeness: and let them have dominion over the fish of the sea, and over the fowl of the air, and over the cattle, and over all the earth." (Genesis 1:26)

One of the biggest lies Satan uses in his arsenal of defense is that God doesn't understand you. Satan has been touting this lie for generations with the intentions of getting us to embrace it. His ultimate aim, though, is to spiritually defeat us, getting us to doubt God. The Word of God says, "We are created in His image and likeness." If we are made in His image and likeness, it stands to reason we also have attributes of God that are both physical and emotional in nature.

For surely it is not angels he helps, but Abraham's descendants. For this reason he had to be made like his brothers in every way, in order that he might become a merciful and faithful high priest in service to God, and that he might make atonement for the sins of the people. Because he himself suffered when he was tempted, he is able to help those who are being tempted. (Hebrews 2:16-18 NIV)

This is a striking picture of Christ identifying with mankind's failures and weaknesses. Christ thought it necessary to lay aside His own Godhood, putting on an "earth suit" to become like us that He might identify with the flesh. This one act alone enabled Him to understand the plight of mankind by allowing Him to experience our weaknesses. In this He showed to us the grace and mercy of the Father. It stands to reason that if we in the flesh suffer rejection, that Jesus who was in the flesh also had the capacity to experience rejection. Christ experienced rejection of His Godhood, His perfection, and His truth, to the point of death on a cross. God's love for us is so great that He chose to send the person He loved the most to be a sacrifice for us. Christ also willingly chose this for Himself because He loved His Father and wanted to bring all of us to the knowledge of Him. This was His gift to the Father. The only way for that to happen was for Christ to enter this world wrapped in human flesh, and in so doing He became just like we are. He experienced pain, joy, happiness, friendship, the love of friends, and eventually physical death.

God cares about what we think and how we feel. His desire is to rescue us, but we limit His ability to help us when we believe He doesn't care. The Spirit of God is a very tangible presence, closer than you may think. His desire is to bring health and healing to our troubled lives. He hears our cries for help.

You know when I sit and when I rise; you perceive my thoughts from afar. You discern my going out and my lying down; you are familiar with all my ways. (Psalm 139:2-3 NIV)

God is intimately and personally aware of every aspect of who we are, for He knows our every thought, and is well acquainted with the emotional pain of hurt and rejection that so easily besets us. We are reminded that, "God is our refuge and strength, a very present help in trouble" (Psalm 46:1). How awesome! He is our defense and our place of hiding. All we have to do is reach out to Him and He'll strengthen us through His Word. Don't buy into the lie that God doesn't care. He cares for us more than we could ever know. If we ask for His help, He'll bring us through.

Chapter 6

Abandonment Issues

And at the ninth hour Jesus cried out in a loud voice, "Eloi, Eloi, lama sabachthani? My God, my God, why have you forsaken me?" (Mark 15:34)

Abandonment makes us feel emotionally lonely and disconnected from others. It is the total withdrawal of love, support, and protection of one to whom we are connected emotionally. When someone we love withdraws their love and support, we find ourselves feeling lost and undone. We may scream out in pain, or we may lash out in retaliation. For Jesus Christ, the brief abandonment of His Father was no different. He was the most perfect and most holy person to ever have walked among us yet He cried out, "My God, my God, why have you forsaken [*abandoned*] me?" (Mark 15:34). The *Vine's Expository Dictionary* translates the word *abandon* to mean "to leave." Jesus became sin for us and because of that, God the Father turned away for a moment. Why did He turn away from His only begotten Son? God is Holy and cannot look upon sin. Christ truly experienced the total leaving of God's presence and felt utterly helpless. He was abandoned during His final moments as He hung on the cross suspended between heaven and Earth. Christ's suffering and death on the cross gave us an opportunity to choose salvation, allowing God to bring healing to our brokenness and all the troubles this life brings.

Deb: When I was abandoned I became angry. I felt no one understood. The previous chapter sums it up so articulately. I became so withdrawn I knocked on the neighbors' door and was welcomed into a sinful "chemical snorting party" which I am sure Satan had prearranged to start my life in the wrong direction. I was lonely and lost. As a Christian, I want to be ready for that lonely abandoned person, counting it a privilege to open my arms and accept them into an environment of scripture and hot tea. I want to help them by leading them to Christ, and listening to them as their life unravels before them.

Janice: There have been times in my life in which the pain of being left was almost too much for me to bear. The pain cut through me like a knife, and I literally felt I was going to be physically ill. You see, I am well acquainted with the feelings that come from emotional and physical abandonment. I was just five years old when I lost one of the most important relationships in my life, my mother. At the age of six my father abandoned me, too, turning my world upside down. Since then I haven't been the same because abandonment changed my expectations. Instead of expecting to be loved

I now expected to be rejected and abandoned. This expectation opened the door for fear to gain an even stronger hold over me.

Unfortunately, we tend to close ourselves off from others who desire to get close. The fear of abandonment causes us to hold them at arm's length. Even in my adult years there have been times I have cut off relationships because I feared emotional abandonment of the relationship. Maybe like me, you're guilty of cutting off relationships to save yourself from being hurt. My friend, the scriptures tell us, "A man [that hath] friends must shew himself friendly: and there is a friend [that] sticketh closer than a brother" (Proverbs 18:24).

Deb: Oh, Janice, dear child, I understand your pain. I can love, accept, and minister to others when I am in control because I trust God and me, but let someone approach me or be tender towards me, then I run and close myself off like a frightened little child. I think that's why during my career God's anointing allowed me so much success because I was in the leadership role. I didn't have to be fearful and afraid.

Janice: I understand the feelings of being afraid to let anyone close. For me though, the worst part of abandonment was I had no security in knowing that anyone loved me or wanted me in their life. I can almost feel the sick feeling come up into my stomach when I remember my father taking me back to the children's home after a visit. He promptly dropped me and my sister off, and didn't seem to notice the tears streaming down our faces as he quickly drove away. We stood watching for the longest time hoping he would turn around and come back for us. But, he never did! I must say that experience left a huge empty hole in my heart. The feelings of dread came over me, and I felt utterly helpless to change the situation. Even worse, I knew in my heart he would never come for me. And I was right! I lived in the children's home from age six until eighteen, when I graduated from High School and left for college.

Abandonment is defined by the Merriam-Webster Dictionary as, "the act of relinquishing any claim or interest in something with the intention of never reclaiming or asserting your rights to it."[13] Physical abandonment is the physical leaving or abandoning of the relationship. In my case the abandonment I experienced was both physical and emotional. Not only did my father abandon me physically, but he left me emotionally, too, giving his parental rights to total strangers. I didn't experience his unconditional love and acceptance because he was never around. I simply existed. So you can say I was abandoned in every sense of the word.

Isn't it sad that our society is one of broken relationships and endless leaving? God never intended for the family to be divided. Satan's plan is to not only divide the family, but wound and maim each member by destroying the family's very foundation. It's unfortunate that the casualties of our broken relationships are our precious children. Children are the most vulnerable and the least considered in the whole dynamic of marriage. They are often left with emotional scars and wounds that don't just heal. We're taught early in our development that if something goes wrong, we can wipe the slate clean and start over. However, it isn't that simple for the ones left behind. Unfortunately, it's not the parents who suffer, it's their children.

Deb: Janice, you and I both know the scars of abandonment. I remember my dad leaving and coming home, leaving and coming back home, until one day he finally left for good. The emotional rollercoaster became a way of life for me. It seems as though in my adult years when things were settled and peaceful, I was more anxious than when our family was in turmoil. I don't know if it was the anxiousness of waiting for the other shoe to drop, or if my spirit had just never been in a calm stable environment and I didn't know how to respond. Janice, I am going to share with you the emotional upset I experienced when my dad would return home. I would be so excited on one hand that he was back and our family was together again, but then on the other hand I knew it wouldn't be long until his rage would be released. Some of my most hurtful and shameful memories, that I've only shared with a handful of people, is that my parents had an unfulfilled marriage and that I slept with my father—my mother slept elsewhere. I was forced to sleep with him from first grade until the age of thirteen or fourteen when he left for the last time.

Janice: One of the biggest lies perpetuated by past generations is the belief that children are resilient and come through unscathed. Yes, it is true children are resilient physically and may quickly bounce back from physical illness, but emotional illness is very different. There are emotional scars left on the heart which can't be seen with the natural eye. These scars surface when they begin to develop relationships of their own. It then becomes apparent the scars never healed.

Parents make the false assumption their children will quickly bounce back, when in fact a gaping wound is seared across their tender, believing hearts. Children are innocent and don't know how to express the heartfelt pain of a parent leaving. They don't know how to explain the deep emotions they are experiencing either. So we parents attempt to put a Band-Aid on their hemorrhaging hearts, filling their days with activities and hoping the awful experience will soon be forgotten. The reality, though, is it's never forgotten and the pain is carried on into adulthood. We then wonder what has happened to our children when a myriad of problems ensues, and they are unable to cope with everyday life.

Deb: When you speak of being sick to your stomach and of the emotional scars left on the heart, I smile and think, "Had I not written this book with you I would have never said out loud that I understand and felt the same depth of loneliness and abandonment." As a matter of fact I was in such denial before counseling, I had never used my name and the word "abandonment" in the same sentence. My outer shell of denial ran so deep I even believed the cool, controlled superficial layers I had piled on top of everything to be an accurate description of me.

Janice: Deb, none of us like to think we are emotionally sick. It's easier to believe we're okay and just the same as everyone else. After being abandoned in the children's home, the biggest issue I struggled with was the fact my father never provided for me in any way. Apparently his provision was hugely important. I took it as a personal blow when he left. I remember seeing young girls and young women with their fathers, making note of the attentiveness their fathers showed them, and my bitter emotions would rise to the top. Why did my father hate me? For a long time I wrestled with these thoughts. I couldn't understand what I had done to make him leave.

Unfortunately, he has never recognized the pain he caused. The person doing the abandoning seldom realizes the anguish and pain resulting from their selfish actions. It's easier to pretend everything is okay and go on without another thought. Often the one doing the abandoning suffers from their own pain and torment, eventually abandoning other relationships when they can't handle them any longer. I have come to realize that our earthly fathers and mothers are finite people who are human and make mistakes. Knowing this, however, doesn't diminish their responsibilities as our parents.

Deb: I couldn't agree more. My father didn't support us either. My mother worked for the same company for twenty one years. Unfortunately the plant later closed and she was forced to get a job in a local restaurant as a cook. Suddenly we were very poor. We drank instant milk made with powder and water, many nights that's what we had for dinner. We lived paycheck to paycheck, rotating the bills we would pay that month. My mother's self-esteem was low, but she did the best she could with the abilities she had. She worked night and day. Her 5'6" thin frame weighed ninety pounds at her most healthy state. After a time she became ill with cancer and her weight spiraled downward until she weighed only sixty-five pounds. I remember her being so miserable and angry. I always cared for her and wanted so much to please her that I forgot about the little girl inside of me.

I have come to know through years of innumerable health problems, what torment and unresolved anger can do to a person. I have suffered from arthritis, ANA Negative Lupus, Colitis, seizures, high blood pressure, female problems, and currently have a menigioma brain tumor. I believe many of my ailments were caused by unresolved childhood trauma. I have been in hospitals all across the country with unexplainable symptoms which were real and were treated. But many physicians scratched their heads and raised their brows because they didn't understand. I ask, "Would I have encountered these diseases if I had not been in emotional bondage?"

Janice: For a long time I hungered to be free from the pain and torment in my life until I eventually turned to the Word of God. I've been saved since about the age of four, but was never taught the importance of living a life totally immersed in Christ. Yes, I read my Bible, but I seemed to be spiritually blind as to the cause of my condition. Instinctively though, I knew somehow in His divine mercy He could deliver me just like He had delivered countless others. I just didn't know how He would deliver me.

Psalm 10:14 speaks of God's true nature, "Thou art the helper of the fatherless." How comforting to know we are not alone, that our Father in heaven is watching and guarding us at all times. Many of you have felt alone your whole lives, but there is one who sticks closer than a brother and that person is the Holy Spirit. The Holy Spirit is a helper that brings relief to our brokenness especially during times of great trial and teaches us what man cannot. He is our defender, defending those who are without help and left without comfort. "But the Comforter, which is the Holy Ghost, whom the Father will send in my name, he shall teach you all things, and bring all things to your remembrance, whatsoever I have said unto you" (John 14:26). He is our advocate and counselor, standing ready to help anyone who asks of Him. His heart is turned toward the rejected and wounded because He desires to be the father or mother you never had. He's reaching out His hands to you now and saying, "Come to me. I have all you need."

Deb: When you talk of emotional torment and turning to the Scriptures later in life, I had a different experience. Growing up I prayed with my sister for my mom and my dad. I was led to Christ by my sister. Although for many years we went our separate ways, the thing we have most in common today is our life long trust in Him. I will say, however, as I reflect back on my life, many times I didn't exercise those scriptures as dramatically as I should have. I hid the loneliness of my heart even from God.

Janice: I'd like to pose a couple of questions for our readers: "Are you dealing with the same wounds of abandonment? Are you afraid of letting others in because you fear they may leave you?" I certainly understand. I, too, put a shield around my heart like your armadillo, where I wouldn't let others into my life. I'll admit it's scary letting anyone into your life with the uncertainty they may leave. My friend, loving others requires taking a risk. We can't live our lives putting a shield of armor around our hearts. Our lives will never be full and happy until we learn the art of loving and giving to others without the expectation of something in return. True love takes a chance even when it knows there's the possibility of rejection. If we are consumed with protecting ourselves from hurt we can expect to live a life of misery. If we choose to close our hearts to the possibility of love, each passing day our wounds deepen until we are completely isolated and alone. I know firsthand the far-reaching effects abandonment has on the human condition, but I also know there is help if we desire to be free.

Do we truly want emotional healing? We have a dream of being free, but that will require us facing life in a new and different way. Are we willing to face the roadblocks that will surely come on the road to getting well? It is through the testing of trials we gain strength, facing each new obstacle with renewed confidence. However, one of the most threatening roadblocks to our healing will be self-pity. We mistakenly believe our lives are somehow harder and more difficult than everyone else's. Arrogance and pride says,

"I'm the only one," when in fact there are millions suffering each day from their own personal pain. Our conversations always speak of ourselves and how dreadful our lives are. "Woe is me" is the theme of our lives, sinking us further into a pit of despair. We would rather talk about what's wrong instead of finding the way out of our misery. We hinder ourselves and stunt any progress when we continually bring up the past. Not only does living in the past keep us thinking unhealthy thoughts, it steals the future we could have. In essence we will find it hard to move forward and change as long as we relive every sordid detail of the past. It's important to acknowledge what happened, but wallowing in self-pity is a trap many fall into that impedes real change.

Deb: That's exciting when you think of emotional healing. Mine has come at the age of fifty-six. For the first time in my life I am able to say that I have been a victim of "abandonment, sexual and physical abuse." I recognize my emotional torment, and I'm accepting the toll it has taken on my life. WOW! I can't believe I said it. It's the first time I've said it out loud in a complete sentence. I almost feel empowered, yet the shame continues to override the freedom I'm feeling right now. I daily need God's help in overcoming these things. I want to find the sweetheart of a daughter that I am in His eyes so that I can be all He desires for me to be. I need Him to continue rescuing and helping me so that I may be heard, justified, and understood.

Janice: Deb, for years I talked about my problems to anyone who would listen. I sought out individuals who were sympathetic to my story, but didn't challenge me to change. I was more interested in having the pity of others than I was in receiving the emotional healing the Lord wanted to grant me. I mulled over and over the awful things that happened to me, rehashing every detail to anyone who would listen. The more I talked about my problems, the longer I stayed entrenched in my troubles. Self-pity is a crutch we use to remain in our sin. We would rather be tormented and miserable than do the hard work it takes to become whole. An attitude of self-pity only ensures we miss opportunities to bring about the changes that would free us.

The fruit of self-pity is whining and complaining. Occasionally circumstances warrant a complaint, but constant whining and crying over small insignificant matters lays bare the root of ingratitude and rebellion. This type of behavior reveals deeper issues within our own hearts. "They despised the pleasant land, they believed not His Word: But murmured in their tents and hearkened not unto the voice of the Lord" (Psalm 106:24-25). The Hebrew word for "murmur" means to grumble and rebel. The Israelites who had God in a cloud by day and a pillar of fire by night, murmured and complained against Him, refusing to believe what He told them. Naturally, like any loving parent, He became dismayed with their behavior and disciplined their rebellion. So they wandered about in the desert for forty years until that generation of whiners and complainers died out. My friend, God's desire is to give us good things, but when we display an ungrateful heart we will not receive anything from God. Stop the murmuring and complaining, give thanksgiving to God, and you'll be surprised at the good that will come to you.

Have you ever noticed little children who manipulate their parents to achieve their wants? The game usually begins with a whine or stomp of the foot to irritate and upset Mommy and Daddy's mood. If that doesn't work, the next step is outright rebellion against authority, throwing a temper tantrum hoping to scare the parents into complying with their wishes. I've even known little children who went as far as holding their breath until they passed out. Of course, the parents don't know how to respond and thought their child had died. Giving into a tantrum only teaches a child that manipulation can help to achieve his desires.

A whining and complaining spirit exposes our ungrateful hearts. We may often take for granted the good in our lives, losing sight of the blessings right in front of us. If only we could see through eyes of faith, I am certain we would see things differently. There have been times in my own life I literally fell on the floor like an eighteen-month-old toddler and threw a temper tantrum. I just couldn't wrap my head around why my life was in the toilet. I thought God wasn't fair in His dealings with me because my hopes and dreams never materialized.

Maybe you are guilty of the same kind of behavior. Maybe you feel wronged and can't understand why your life is headed in the wrong direction. ***Blaming God never changes our circumstances.*** I realize I am the real source of my own problems, and it is up to me to take inventory of my own attitudes and behaviors. I want to challenge you to do the same and take substantial inventory of your life. Just like me, you may find you are your own worst enemy.

Deb: I suppose while I never was able to mention my problems out loud before, I did whine and complain about my sickness and was focused way too much on being sick. In the early years I was too busy praying for others that I didn't consider praying for myself. Now that I know the root cause to the many years of problems, I'm getting counseling from a couple of very special Christian people who God has placed in my life. For the first time I am allowing God to heal the small, young, innocent, sweet, awesome child that lives within me. I want to remind our readers that it was this year that I asked God for total healing: mentally, physically, spiritually, and emotionally. Daily I have repeated, "My God is healing me."

Longing to Belong

Janice: The truth of my dad's selfishness was uglier than I ever imagined. Raising four small children was a task he had no intentions of undertaking. The weight of parental responsibility wasn't going to tie him down, his plans didn't include parenting. He would find a way to fix everything. He was used to getting his way and this time would be no different. He would say or do whatever necessary to make it happen. My father has always been good at making excuses for his life; someone else was always to blame. This was his M.O., his *modus operandi* or mode of operation.

While plans were being made about our future, we were tossed from foster home to foster home. The Bureau of Children and Family Services provided assistance to my father, and helped to radically change the direction of our lives forever. The decision finally came down to put us in a children's home. I don't know what excuse he used to convince them, but whatever it was it worked like a charm. For years I wrestled with the question of why he left. It made no sense to me until many years later I realized he made the choice to leave us. The choices he made had nothing to do with our unworthiness, but everything to do with his own selfish desires. He always put himself first, so walking away wasn't that difficult to do. Somehow he was able to reason that putting us away was in our best interest. I suppose this was the only way he could sleep at night.

Those of us who have been abandoned emotionally and physically feel we never fit in with anyone or belong anyplace. Loneliness is our closest companion, even when we're in a crowd of people. We put on a smile to benefit others, but inwardly we're empty and ache for acceptance. True happiness eludes us and appears to be out of our reach. We strive to make some sense of our lives, but openness about our thoughts and feelings are risks we're not willing to take, so we keep our hurts locked inside. We dare not share who we are because chances are we'll be rejected again, or someone will use our wounds as a weapon to hurt us. I've had this happen to me more often than I wish to count. We long to trust those closest to us, but often they inflict the most damage, thinking they are helping us overcome our problems. Instead, they're helping to deepen our wounds. If we're not handled with gentle love and kindness, we'll again withdraw into our own world, closing ourselves off from those who hurt us and even those who can help us.

Emotionally twisted people are seldom understood by healthy individuals. Being the tangled mess we are, we're often criticized and misjudged harshly for our erratic behavior. Sadly, misinformed people only add wood to the fire and unknowingly inflict more wounds. This is why we desperately need the Lord's help. We must understand Christ came to redeem us. "The Spirit of the Lord is upon me, because he hath anointed me to preach the gospel to the poor; he hath sent me to heal the broken-hearted, to preach deliverance to the captives, and recovering of sight to the blind, to set at liberty them that are bruised" (Luke 4:18). Christ came to heal the broken in heart, mind, soul, spirit, and body, and all those who have been emotionally bruised, crushed by life, and broken by circumstances. Praise God, we have someone who loves us unconditionally and without pretense. The love and acceptance we have hungered for our whole lives is now right in front of us. What are we going to do with it?

Deb: You have said a mouthful, my friend. I truly have never belonged anywhere my entire life. You might say, "How so?" All those years lecturing in front of groups of thousands of people didn't fill the void in my heart. What I have to be thankful for is His timing, His grace, and His mercy. I wouldn't change one thing about my life. I feel I have been in grad school since I turned nineteen. Every year has been sweeter, and every experience He has afforded me more precious. I have grown closer and closer to the Lord all the time as He has provided more and more mercy. He has taught me what I have in a Christian Spirit-filled and faithful husband who loves me more than anyone deserves. To still be dating and in love in your mid-fifties tells a sweet story. My children, their love and respect for me blow my mind. I made so many mistakes along the way. Being raised by myself (literally), I didn't have parental examples. So many basic qualities a good mother possesses didn't come by observing. It either came naturally or not at all. So I am blessed to be so loved and cared for in such a special way. Everything that happened to me as a child is nothing by comparison of what God provided to me **most** of my life. I stand amazed at His goodness!

Chapter 7

Allow Him to Change You

Be still, and know that I am God; I will be exalted among the nations, I will be exalted in the earth. (Psalm 46:10 NIV)

Deb: Change is occurring all around us every day. It is much like visiting someone you haven't seen for a long time. Their age, weight, makeovers or lack of self-care is magnified, but when we live next door we do not see the subtle changes in people or situations. We are always amazed when things become evident. Our state of affairs in our country **blows** me away. I often wonder when we became so careless. Were we simply "out to lunch" caring for so many other concerns, or are we the Americans we have been "dubbed" by the Canadians and Europeans?

When my husband and I travelled abroad to adopt our fourth child, sweet Maggie, we were warned of the reputation we Americans have overseas. We were cautioned that many Europeans hate the

American people. I was enlightened with statements such as we are a society of self-entitled, paranoid, arrogant, unsophisticated, fat, lazy, vulgar, greedy, racist, spoiled-rich, ignorant, non-giving, stubborn, stupid, humorless, loud, obnoxious, gum-chewing, self-centered, and uncouth, as well as obsessed with sex, ourselves, and celebrities. I quickly went to our defense. I love America and her people. But the more I look around and look inwardly at myself, I realize that we all have become less than what our forefathers taught, and we are a nation so blessed that we have become spoiled. I would love to turn my anger on them shouting, "You change," but instead I will suggest in the name of Jesus, "We change." Notice I say, "We." I have so many ways that need to be visited and changed. We have lived a life of favor, therefore simply becoming less because we have had more.

There is a group of college kids whom I fell in love with. They have travelled extensively in search of God. Their goal is to be the Christians they need to be, but with a privileged background and Christian values passed on without true biblical teaching, they simply didn't feel they were doing all they could for God. They have a DVD titled, *Beware of Christians.* It is heavy but beautiful and will change the next generation. I love how they are living out one of my favorite quotes, "Be the change you want to see in the world" (Mahatma Gandhi).

I have purposely taken some time out to listen to God, to discover what He wants. I know that He is in control when I fully surrender. "Be still and know that I am God!" (Psalm 46:10). For me that scripture is a mouthful. For the past year I've been in constant prayer. It has seemed like six or seven years being quiet and still, and it has nothing to do with my time. It has been through this alone time that the Lord has ministered healing to me.

You see, the plan several years ago was to retire, work for God, and run the non-profit we had already started, "Live to give...a God Thing," which I did. It has the sole purpose of helping young people know Christ, both here and abroad. I also started a line of jean jackets in which we collected jean jackets for rehabilitation. We added new colors and cuffs, selling them for an orphanage in Kenya. We had plans to open a modern-day soup kitchen.

After all the final plans were drawn up and we were months from opening, I heard the Lord say, "These are your plans for LTG, not Mine."

He always gives me confirmation. The place where we had planned to put the soup kitchen was rented by someone else. No Worries! There will be another place, I thought, and it quickly came up or I made it happen. Once again we lost the space.

God plainly said, "Quit working Me into your plans and let Me have all of you for Myself."

I pouted all summer that God was in charge and I wasn't.

The next thing that happened is my husband said, "Deb, (while we were at our summer home) I think you should stay and put the kids in the Christian school here."

The old, prior to October 2, 2011 Deb said, "Why would you suggest that? God doesn't want that! He wants us together. He would never want a family split."

I quickly became outraged and all kinds of past junk came out such as, "Do you want to have an affair?"

Taken directly out of my past, I stewed, because my father wasn't faithful to my mother, and my father's father wasn't faithful to his mother. This was generational sin. I'm not implying my husband had any intentions of doing wrong; it just meant there was still a precious wounded child within me. "I" fought! Don remained calm. Our last two children are in the Christian school in Hilton Head.

Janice: Deb, I think most of us cringe at the very thought of another person taking control of our lives. The term "surrender" conjures up frightening images in our minds. We don't normally associate surrender with something positive, but rather something negative. For example, in the past surrender meant someone took advantage of us, or used us, thus leaving a scar on our trusting heart. Someone we loved hurt us, and we just can't take the chance of feeling that kind of pain and rejection again. Instead, we erect a wall around our hearts to keep others out, including a loving God. Questions race through our minds like, "What are the chances I'll be hurt again if I totally abandon myself to God? Or what will I have to give up?" Total surrender requires trust on our part and taking the risk that God will not fail us. The choice to trust Him is ours to make. He is a gentleman and will never force Himself on us or anyone.

"Now faith is the substance of things hoped for, the evidence of things not seen" (Hebrews 11:1). The *Strong's Concordance* says, "Faith is a strong conviction or belief that Jesus is the Messiah through whom we obtain eternal salvation and the character of one who can be relied on."[14]

"Let us draw near with a true heart in full assurance of faith, having our hearts sprinkled from an evil conscience, and our bodies washed with pure water" (Hebrews 10:22). Notice the words "full assurance," meaning a total confidence in God's willingness, ability, and power to take care of us in every circumstance. Whether our needs are emotional, physical or spiritual, God is able and willing to watch over and keep His own.

What can we expect when we put our complete confidence in God? First, we can enjoy a freedom in our minds that comes in knowing He will take care of us. Secondly, we experience a profound freedom as we rest in the full assurance that He has pledged His faithfulness to us. Lastly, the ending result is a deep abiding trust in God that is unshakable. I'll admit learning to trust God hasn't been easy for me, and I would be lying if I said I've never doubted Him. But over the years I have grown in my trust, and I now rest in the assurance that all is well even when everything around me is falling apart. Learning to trust God will mean a deliberate surrendering of our wills to God without trying to reassert our own control.

Deb: When we look at our individual lives, are we the change we want to see or do we live more by, "An eye for an eye and a tooth for a tooth"? (Leviticus 24:20). It seems to me that we miss the message here when we feel we have a right to retaliation. This is a verse which has been quoted by those outside the church for generations. We live with retaliation and vengeance as a stronghold in our lives. If you don't believe me wait until your spouse criticizes you the next time. Immediately, we jump to a childlike behavior or the sport of "one-up-man-ship," always able to fire back the loudest and strongest. I fight this animal with my own defensiveness and desire to not be hurt.

What if we awoke every morning and before we got out of bed, wrote down our desire to be the change in the world we would like to see. What if we determine to love like Jesus when someone puts us down, and walk away with a smile on our face as though nothing happened. We hurt Him when we choose wrong over right, bad over good, invoking pain on a worker who has stood at the drive through window all day long and makes a simple fixable mistake. We are loaded and ready for fire. Christians, shame on you. Non-Christians know that we (Christians) are trying to get it right. We aren't perfect but we are trying! The Word of God is full of angry people who got it right with God. If they can make things right with people, we can do the same. We are all part of God's amazing plan for good. What He does ask us to do is found in Micah 6:8. What does the Lord require of you and me but "to do justice and to love kindness and to walk humbly with your God?" Sounds easy enough or does it?

We are human and live in a carnal world, so how can we stay in God's plan? First, start by spending more time living in the spiritual world. This is an opportunity to point out the need for us to spend more time in His Word. The Word of God ultimately changes us to become the change we want to see. The Psalmist said it so well, "With my whole heart I have sought you. Your word I have hidden in my heart so that I might not sin against you" (Psalm 119:10-11). Talk about being changed. Be prepared to store up those scriptures, they are the tools needed for life's battles.

I'm reminded of a song by Jimmie McKnight, whose words are timeless. His remarkable poetry shows his heart for God, and shows us the change God desires to give us.

Tossed about by life's battles, all my hopes were sinking fast. This sinful life that I was living, Lord I knew it could not last. Then I went down to the Potters house, I placed this vessel into His hand and on His wheel of grace and mercy He made me over again! Yes, I've been to the Potters' house, His hands of mercy molded me. He sent me forth when He was finished so that this entire world can see that He can mend a broken vessel it matters not what shape it is in. Yes I've been to the Potters house I've been made over again. If your life has no meaning, the storms have taken that toll on you, with your vessel in many pieces, you don't know just what to do, Oh, please come with me to the Potters house, you'll be amazed

at His ability to make you over again. Jimmie McKnight

Oh, my! I feel chill bumps knowing He loves me, and has the ability to wipe out the old and bring in the new. God is excited about giving second chances, helping us put our vessels back together so we are pleasing unto Him. That being said, the change we want to see begins with a serious spiritual makeover. Botox isn't needed for this girl because I'm talking about a change from the inside out where true beauty shines through. Oh, the beauty that is awaiting us at the Potter's house.

Janice: You know sanctification takes time. I grew up defending myself against children who not only provoked me through name calling, but made me feel inferior. I just wanted to crawl under a rock and disappear. If anyone had a reason to lash out in retaliation, I would say it was me. Although I've been saved since I was very young, when I got angry I wanted to act out in my flesh and knock someone's lights out. Learning to love unlovely people, including myself, has been a challenge. We all want someone to pay for the injustice we feel has been done to us. Unfortunately, some of us do retaliate and this doesn't bring glory to God. It only reveals our weaknesses, and ruins our Christian testimony before others. I do want to be the positive change that helps to change the world. My prayer is for more of God's unconditional love to be seen and felt through me.

"God, let me be Your hands, let me be Your feet, let me speak the words that You speak, and let Your love shine through me. Yes! Let the change begin with me!"

Deb: Shhhhhh! "Be still, and know that I [am] God: I will be exalted among the heathen, I will be exalted in the earth" (Psalm 46:10). When people say, "SHHHH!" it's amazing how it quiets us. We have been brought up that way with a universal shushing if you will. I have grown closer to Him, learning more when I am quiet and still before Him. When I take time just to be, the Lord speaks **real** peace to me. Over the years I have purchased every book on breathing, relaxing, and being good to myself, but none of them have ever gotten me to the place the Holy Spirit wanted me to be. For those of you who know me, you are laughing because being quiet is not a part of my natural demeanor. Oh, there were numerous ways God would get my attention, but I never really took to the "quiet thing." Now I want to drive down the street with my windows down saying, "I get it," "I finally get it!" Get what? I get the "quiet thing." Oh, how He then opens me up, feeds me, encourages me, edifies me, and strengthens me. I am so lucky to have found true quiet time with my Savior where He molds me and makes me His own.

Don't get me wrong. I have, for as long as I can remember, awakened early to have my time with Him. In addition to my regular prayer life, in recent years I have taken scriptures about rising up early and have applied them to my prayer life. "O God, thou [art] my God; early will I seek thee: my soul thirsts for thee, my flesh longs for thee in a dry and thirsty land, where no water is" (Psalm 63:1). I have in recent year's surrendered time to just be "still," listening to Him and stopping my self-imposed hustle and bustle. I rotate times of praising Him for an hour with times of employing the skill of being still, listening, and knowing that He is God. Practicing this kind of prayer life allows me to get out of God's way, eliminating the boundaries I may try to place upon Him. His best is better than ours.

In life, one of the most flattering forms of a compliment is when folks listen to you. You might assume they feel what you say has importance, but in a seminar, church service, or classroom the highest form of flattery is to listen intently. It saddens me that within our personal relationships we run from listening. We bore easily. We finish our loved ones sentences before they finish their actual formation of the thought they are presenting. Just today, while eating in a restaurant, I pointed out to my daughter the actions of a man sitting at the table next to us.

I posed a question to her, "What do you observe the man sitting next to us doing, that his wife might not be pleased about?"

She answered immediately, "Texting."

This opened a teaching opportunity for me to testify to her how respectful her father is to me. I shared with her how our life in our mid-fifties is just as exciting as when we first met in our twenties. I further explained to her the importance of respect in a relationship. Years ago if you had company in your home, you never answered the phone when it rang or if you did, you told the caller you would return their call later. Yes, we do the same thing to our Lord and Savior. We get in His way by not listening. Our spiritual eyes are opened when we are quiet. We then can hear His call and what He has in store for us. **Listen!** God is calling your name. I feel by listening to God and waiting upon Him, we will in fact find ourselves in peaceful situations. Many people run around demanding peace from God or telling Him how peace looks to them. But His Word tells us, "My peace I give to you, I do not give to you as the world gives, Do not let your hearts be troubled and do not let them be afraid" (John 14:27).

Janice: Deb, you are so right about us needing to remove the distractions that crowd out God's voice in our lives. Getting quiet and still is necessary to hear His will and direction. We need His thoughts daily to strengthen and encourage us, especially on those days we feel very much alone. That's why it's so important to get God's Word planted deeply within our hearts, so we can draw upon His words of life for ourselves and others. It's so easy to neglect our relationship with Him, especially when the television is going, the phone is ringing, or someone needs our help. Deliberately taking the time to not only pray, but to actively listen to His voice is vitally important in our Christian walk. When two people are involved in a conversation, they usually give each other a turn to speak. The same should be true with our Heavenly Father. We need to give Him the opportunity to speak to us about His plans and His direction for our lives before interjecting our own thoughts and plans. "Rest in the Lord, and wait patiently for him" (Psalm 37:7). The word "rest" simply means to "be still" and wait. This means we are not to run ahead of Him, but wait for Him to answer—He will answer if we listen.

Deb: If I come before Him to just listen, without bringing up my troubles and complaints, He can speak all He wants because I am open to His voice. He knows our every need and knows exactly what to speak and when to speak it. If He has numbered every hair on our heads then He knows exactly what we need before we ask. Being quiet really pays!

Going back to my prayer on October 2, 2011, I said repeatedly, "I surrender all." I prayed to God, "Please open my heart and soul, dissecting it as though I was having a MRI scan. Please slice it and dice it into a million pieces and heal any dark spots by revealing them to me. I offer you my secrets and all that I have hidden so deeply in my heart from You and from myself, Lord Jesus." I told my precious Lord and Savior that I wanted to trust Him with all of me—finally! I am 57 years old, and Janice, I can honestly tell you it was this year that I finally stepped out in total faith, being led by the Holy Spirit to completely trust Him for the first time.

I posted a proclamation on my bathroom mirror that reads, "From this day forward God is healing me emotionally, physically, mentally, and spiritually." I pray this numerous times throughout the day, praising Him for all He is doing in my life. I have forgiven my father numerous times for abandoning me and for his abuse of me. Today, I choose to forgive him again. I will pass along forgiveness today and repeat the process on a daily basis as I start anew each day. Life is a process and forgiveness is a journey. My prayer for today is, "Lord, I ask daily for You to help me remember to praise You that generational sin has been torn down in Your name. Today, it stops with me. You hear me and You alone have delivered me and redeemed me and are in the process of healing me."

Sin and Iniquity

Janice: One topic we seldom hear mentioned in some churches anymore is the subject of sin and iniquity. We can't talk about allowing Him to change us without mentioning sin and iniquity. They are in essence the root causes of all the problems we suffer in this life. The word "iniquity" is so important to getting our relationship right with God that it is mentioned some seventy-nine times in the Bible. King David was acutely aware of the extreme dominating power iniquity played in his life and its affects when not confessed. In his failure to confess his iniquity, God turned a deaf ear to his pleas. "If I regard iniquity in my heart, the Lord will not hear [me]" (Psalm 66:18).

Deb: Think of the importance of opening our hearts daily and asking the Holy Spirit in for a review of where we stand with our iniquity. Literally, like a dorm mom, write me up where I'm short.

Janice: Recently I purchased a book titled, *Iniquity,* written by Dr. Ana Mendez Ferrell. What she says in this book is astounding. My eyes were opened to my true spiritual condition, unveiling the truth behind the troubles I have faced all my life. She writes:

"Iniquity is what the Bible calls the body of sin." She goes on to say, "Iniquity is intrinsically tied to the spiritual world of darkness, and it is there the devil binds us with the curses from our ancestors. It is in this place the legal basis of sickness are rooted and transmitted from the parents to their children and from the children to their grandchildren. It is also here where Satan's legal right is granted to rob, to destroy, and even to kill us."[15]

In the above statement, we see how the baton of iniquity is passed from one generation to the next. The painful wounds inflicted on us were not of our own doing, but we inherited them through iniquity as punishment for the sins of our fathers. All egregious actions perpetrated against us were conceived first in iniquity, then played out by a family member, by which we became the victims of injustice. Although we are innocent victims of injustice, we are still accountable before God to break the power of those sinful acts of unrighteousness. First, we must examine our heart with all honesty, allowing God to point out to us the areas of darkness and sin that need extermination. Secondly, we must turn and repent for our iniquities and the iniquities of our ancestors, applying the blood of Jesus to break the curses off our lives and our children's lives. As a result of our obedient behavior, the channel of communication is opened between us and God, allowing His blessings to flow towards us. Choosing to ignore them allows the same sinful behavior to continue on to the next generation.

Deb: Janice that's beautiful and much like I refer to in my "come to Jesus" moment on October 2, 2011. I love it!

Janice: Iniquity was behind the suicide of my mother, iniquity was behind my father abandoning me, and iniquity was behind rejection. "Iniquity is the full embodiment of all sin in our lives," says Dr. Ana Mendez Ferrell.[16] Iniquity is behind abuse, rape, murder, lust, violence, hatred, greed, trust in man, love of money, bitterness, sexual molestation, addictions of all kinds, and many more sins. That's why it's necessary to not only repent for our own personal sins, but for the sins of our ancestors thereby breaking the generational curses from passing to our children. I never want my children to experience the emotional pain of abandonment or rejection that has riddled my life. I want to stop once and for all the passage of these sins, and more importantly I want to be in right standing with my Heavenly Father. I want the channel of communication between me and my God to remain free and clear from sin and debris.

Deb: How excited are you about change? "Not very," I imagine. Many people have an issue with change. I think of all of the sport enthusiasts who cheer until they are hoarse for their teams. Are we cheering above a whisper for the Great I Am? I believe it is all about Jesus.

As I sat patiently waiting for my husband the other morning at an outdoor breakfast café, a couple of people approached me with, "What do you do?"

Surprising even myself, I resounded with Christ on my lips and said, "I work for Jesus."

After they went back to breakfast and tried to ignore me, I laughed to myself and thought what a great way to discourage idle chatter on the airplane. Why are we so afraid to mention His name? I get it! I looked like a goofus, but I was proud that my zealous outburst even made me think. Who am I? Whose am I? And what is my purpose?

Then my husband came to the table and I told him, "We are weird."

We laughed and he said, "You are weird!"

We had a wonderful breakfast. I may never understand why those words came out so abruptly, but He does. If looking like a total Jesus freak at that moment was my calling, them I must obey. I do love Jesus and want to work for Him the rest of my life. I am ashamed I didn't do more all along. Craig Groeschel refers to us as part-time lovers. That is the visual I need to carry on with my full-time approach. After I find myself not celebrating God in church to the fullest because I am concerned people think it is either showing off or over the top, I ask myself, "Why do I care?" My worship should be so personal with the Lord of lords and the Creator of my universe that I don't even see anyone but Him. I want to be free of myself so I can clearly see the freedom that we now have to worship Him, though we may not have that freedom forever.

Janice: Deb, you know King David worshipped God with his whole being and came under the scrutiny of his wife. He was so in love with God, he didn't care what the congregation or even his wife thought of him. I think this is the way we should worship our King, with total abandon regardless of the raised eyebrows and whispers we get from others. It should come as no surprise to us that we're laughed at and made fun of for the love and adoration we freely exhibit during worship.

Change is a word that concerns a lot of people, while some of us are always ready for change as we bore easily. The Bible is full of requests from God for His people to change. "Therefore if any man [be] in Christ, [he is] a new creature: old things are passed away; behold all things are become new" (1 Corinthians 5:17). Change is inevitable if we are growing in Christ. As I ponder change, I realize people are looking for social change, environmental change, immigrant law change, healthcare change, and political change. There is even a change website, www.change.org! From Face book, to Twitter, to blogging, to dictionary.com where we can look up transform, convert, and the witch that turned the prince into a toad—all talking about major transformation. We resist change because we are satisfied being in a "groove." Let me encourage you to do one thing each month to promote change or action in your relationship with Christ!

Deb, speaking of change, I can't believe people are pouring into theaters to see *War Hunger Games*. Have we gone completely nuts—watching kids kill each other? You can't convince me that our society is any further along than during the Roman Empire times in which there was so much violence. Schools are now taking kids to watch this movie and the audiences stand up and applaud. There is no reason why we should be watching this kind of entertainment, least of all, letting our kids watch it. We parents are too busy to get involved. I hate to be an activist or be negative, but really? Come on, parents! We are watching our children being led to the slaughter.

Deb: It is people who have money who are fighting over this. I would collapse if my daughter even remotely had an interest in seeing this. My God! Are we as a society this lame? The amount of money this industry makes could go instead to doing good works and making a positive change in our world. They are acting like poorly reared, ungodly children. All this is rude, crude, and socially unacceptable behavior in the name of the almighty dollar, and for what? If only they would turn to God and use all their money to implement a program based on the authority of Christ and teach the next generation how to behave. STOP! Hit your knees folks, let's have a major revival of America and reaffirm what she stands for. I am not amused, nor am I amazed anymore. The book *Weird* by Craig Groeschel says it all: "The new normal is what this show is about and *Weird* is what we as Christians that seek His will live for. I am gladly weird in a God way, and I hope to stay that way."[17]

Until we turn off our televisions, stop buying violent games for our children, and stop supporting the local movie theaters that show movies with kids killing other kids in the name of friends, our kids will continue to be led about as a sheep being led to the slaughter. Thank God, I have a Shepherd who keeps me safe, who is willing to lay across the fence to protect me as well as encourage me to make wise decisions. He helps me to rise above all of this absolute nonsense giving me wisdom to make right choices for me and my family.

When will we pull together and do something? I think so many Christians are too busy worrying about the **big** sins, such as perverse sexuality, adulterous affairs, and whatever gossip is running its course in the grapevine. Christian women, we need to bond together in the spirit of the Holy One and go after souls for Christ.

Chapter 8

The Power of Forgiveness

The righteous shall flourish like the palm tree: he shall grow like a cedar in Lebanon. Those that be planted in the house of the LORD shall flourish in the courts of our God. (Psalm 92:12-13)

Deb: Yesterday while I sat in church, the words from the pulpit were like a dagger penetrating my soul. The words rang out like the annoying sound of breaking glass in my ears. "Rooted anger and resentment," cried the preacher. The hair stood up on the back of my neck and I knew he was talking to me. You see, I have done a great job of pushing the pain of bitter unforgiveness down so no one could see it. I pretended for years that my pain didn't exist, and did a wonderful job of loving God in the midst of it all. I have gleaned so much knowledge and revelation over the past several months which have brought me to a stark reality; we Christians are as guilty as unbelievers in ignoring Him.

As I listened to the pastor's brilliant message, in the back of my mind I thought about the root system of a plant. As I sat there contemplating the plant, I saw the many veins stemming off the root, and how they forked left and right just like a crooked road. I imagined that my heart and soul were wrapped up by the many branches and shoots, almost choking me from the resentment and smoldering anger I had held onto most of my life. After years of dealing with my emotional entrapment, and the many years of built-up self-pity, resentment, and outbursts of wrath, it was really hard to identify the original cause of all the pain. Quite frankly, it has taken me months to get back to the "original sore spot" or the "original place" where it all began.

Janice: Deb, that sermon sounds like one we all need.

Deb: I read an interesting article on the internet by Jim Swanson, *Evidence of Design*, which I would like to share that explains this principle so clearly.

The root system of a palm tree is unique. Most trees have branching roots that grow smaller and smaller the further they are from the taproot. The palm roots are the same size at the stem or base. This makes the tree difficult to pull up. It also means the roots will grow deep into the ground, getting nourishment that is not available on the surface. David said the blessed man is "like a tree planted by the rivers of water that bringeth forth his fruit in his season" (Psalm 1:3). God also commands us to "take root downward, and bear fruit upward" (Isaiah 37:31). Most tree trunks are made up of dead wood while the living part, the cambium layer, is just inside the bark. This makes it easy for animals to 'girdle' a tree, nibbling the bark around the bottom and thus killing it. The palm, on the other hand, has living wood throughout. Therefore, damage to the truck has little or no affect. This and the strong root system allow it to weather hurricane force storms because it bends with the wind without breaking. When our lives are rooted in Christ (Colossians 2:6-7), the storms of life have a way of spiritually strengthening us. Fruit trees normally decrease in fruit production as they grow older. Palm trees do not bear fruit at all until they are mature. This takes up to fifty years. But as the palm tree ages, the fruit grows sweeter. Consider this promise: "They shall still bring forth fruit in old age; they shall be fat and flourishing" (Psalm 92:14). God does not want us to become less fruitful in old age. Instead the fruit of our lives should increase and become sweeter as the years pass.[18]

Janice: I agree with Psalm 92:14—as you and I know, it is so true. My desire has been to produce fruit as we journey together, helping others with our testimony, Deb.

Deb: As I write this, Janice, my heart is open to the Holy Spirit. If it were up to me, I would close this laptop and move on as I have done so many times in the past—pushing down my own pain and ignoring the little girl who cries out to be heard. Let me share with you that there are no "martyr awards," and there are no "crowned jewels" awaiting those who quietly suffer. The "fake it till you make it" mentality that I taught for so many years doesn't work when the One who made us His own is calling us to put our total trust in Him by baring our secrets and shame. All He wants from us is that we be completely honest and open with Him, opening ourselves up for Him to heal every heartache and pain so that we can be His disciples, working for Him. Until He heals us of our deep painful memories, which have been stored up as emotional baggage, we can't fully surrender to Him. Dr. Lynette Weist describes it best in her Sunshine analogy where she sees God as the sun which is always shining. However, our baggage of unforgiveness is represented by the clouds blocking the brightness of the sun. I am a visual learner and this visual works beautifully for me as I work on weeding and clearing out the areas of my life that block the rays of God's sunshine (Son). The next time anyone says they wish the sun would come out remember it is out; the clouds are just blocking its brightness.

Janice: Inner healing comes as we learn forgiveness. Without it, we'll waste years dealing with the same issues over and over, which create the yo-yo effect we experience with unresolved issues. As a result, these issues remain in the forefront of our thoughts. Unforgiveness interferes with us changing and growing because we justify our sin and our reasons for holding on to the past. It's easy to convince ourselves that forgiveness is old-fashioned and outdated, but the truth, however painful it may be, is that unforgiveness is the cause of why we can't be emotionally well. It is the key to our emotional and spiritual health. We may have reason to be unforgiving, but without forgiveness we will remain fragmented individuals, not only in our spirit but our bodies, too. The cancer of bitter unforgiveness will continue to spread until it consumes our relationship with God and with others.

Bitterness is an intense contempt and animosity towards another, exposing the root of hatred imbedded deep within our own hearts. It is eating away at us like a cancer until everything is filled with poisonous venom, destroying everything good in our lives. In fact we are imprisoned when we hold onto past wrongs and hurts. The person who has wronged us appears to suffer very little if at all. In our bitterness we want our abuser to suffer just as much or more than we did at their hands. The righteous thing to do, however, would be to show mercy and pray for their salvation. It's true they wounded and hurt us, but it's evident they are depraved and need God in their lives just as much as we do. We can't have this attitude in us unless we've truly embraced forgiveness. It is sad, however, that the abuser is seldom aware of the injustice they have committed, and it's possible they may never know.

I want to explain to you in easy terms just how the effect of unforgiveness plays out in our everyday lives. I'll use a metaphor showing how bitterness and forgiveness are intertwined like a wisteria vine.

Naturally, we know trees have roots systems and must be watered to keep them healthy and growing. As a result of the nourishment it receives, a tree yields fruit according to the type of tree it is. If it's an orange tree then it produces oranges; if it's an apple tree it produces apples. You get the idea. Then let's say this particular tree with its root system is a bitterness tree. The fruit produced from this type of tree will always be unforgiveness because a bitterness tree can only produce after its kind. The water used to nourish the tree represents our bitterroot memories.

Unforgiveness is the fruit, bitterness the root, and its nourishment represents our bitterroot memories. Bitterroot memories are those memories we continually think about that have caused us a lot of emotional hurt and pain. As you can see, each one plays a role in fortifying and giving strength to the other. Bitterness gives legs and feet to unforgiveness, and bitterroot memories keep them alive by reminding us of all the wrongs done to us by others. When we refuse to confront unforgiving thoughts, and continue watering this tree with bitter memories, it continues to grow producing rotten fruit in our lives. Let me say with boldness that we don't have to keep our pain. We can give it up right now. The choice is ours to make.

Deb: My life has not been perfect to say the least. For the past fifty years I've known my life was abnormal in so many ways, and that I needed healing. At the tender age of five, I thought perhaps I had been adopted, because I just never felt I belonged anywhere. Now, at age 57, I'm wishing I had been adopted. I must say I am forgiving my father daily. The process has been a long one, and I thought many times that I should have finished dealing with this part of my life, continuing to move forward. I am acutely aware that if I had not suffered the childhood trauma in which my sexual boundaries were compromised, as well as the emotional and physical abuse I suffered, I wouldn't be the person He is molding me into.

As a young person, I used to go off on people for behaviors I found appalling. Once I remember being at a local Arlans store, which is similar to a Kmart or Wal-Mart, and a woman and her husband were fiercely beating their little dog. I was all of sixteen years old. I angrily walked up to them, took their dog, cuddled him, and told them I was taking the dog to protect him from them. I'm not sure how I walked into that situation, but my rage and pain was equal or greater than theirs. I thought, "They dare not mess with me or it's going be a bad day." I walked out of that store with their dog. To me it was important that I intervene to save a helpless animal.

That is only one of the many angry outbursts I've had over the years. Some were heroic while others were completely embarrassing, painful, and just shameful moments in which I shall be eternally sorry for. In my book, *Good Morning, Good Night 99 Days to Your Spiritual Recovery,* I asked the question, "Who have you wronged?" Then I made the suggestion of picking up the telephone and making it right with the other person. To this day I barely remember writing that and a year from now I will probably have forgotten some of these words God anointed me to write in this book. But I'm writing them because there is someone out there who needs to hear the truths written between these pages. God is calling you! When I read the directive, I picked up the phone and made the call to apologize for my bad behavior from nearly forty years ago. It was so self-healing and a Godly conversation.

Janice: "Let all bitterness, wrath, anger, and evil speaking be put away from you, with all malice: And be ye kind one to another, tenderhearted, forgiving one another, even as God for Christ's sake has forgiven you" (Ephesians 4:31-32). Making the choice to release our bitterness and pain opens wide the door to forgiveness, and we find hope and emotional freedom is ours for the taking. As we continue walking down the path of forgiveness, past wounds begin to heal, and we find the inner healing and peace we've longed for all our lives.

The Power of Emotions

Janice: Emotions are strong feelings that influence our outlook on life. They are neither good nor bad, but act as an inward barometer measuring the way we think and feel about people and situations. For example, anger is a normal emotion we all experience at some time in our lives. The aptitude to be angry isn't sinful in and of itself, but rather it's our mishandling of anger that draws us into sin. We are taught in the Scriptures, "Be angry, and sin not: let not the sun go down on your wrath" (Ephesians 4:6). Learning the art of managing our emotions without sinning against another teaches us to handle them in a calm dignified Christ like manner. Many times in Scripture Christ was angry, but He never deprived anyone of their dignity. In our culture, it is commonplace to see angry, degenerate people cursing others in a fit of rage, stripping them of their self-worth. Maybe this kind of behavior describes you. If so, you can change that right now. All that's needed is to lay aside your bitterness and anger. Let it go! Rebuild the relationships you've torn apart through bitter angry words by replacing them with words of love and kindness.

I can't emphasize enough the importance of choosing our words wisely. Words have power to build up or destroy another. "If any man among you seems to be religious, and bridleth not his tongue, but deceiveth his own heart, this man's religion [is] vain" (James 1:26). To paraphrase what is being said in this verse, "Those of you who supposedly serve God but can't restrain your tongue, are deceived. Your service to God is pointless and useless." The word vain simply means devoid of truth. But you might say, "I serve on the deacon board at church, I pay my tithes every week, and I feed the hungry." My friend, please listen to me carefully. Religious activity doesn't guarantee salvation any more than separation from sin makes one holy. You can participate in all the religious activity your heart desires, but it's the inability to control your tongue that is leading you away from God and into deception.

Deb: "Just then a woman who had been subject to bleeding for twelve years came up behind him and touched the edge of his cloak"

(Matthew 9:20 NIV). BAM! Forgiven! That's how I want the entire process to be as I am sure you do, too. "To forgive or not to forgive is the question," not for God of course, but for us. He stands ready to forgive. His forgiveness is BAM! We, on the other hand, not so much so. We find forgiveness as difficult as surrendering control. Perhaps they are more closely related than we think. Forgiving ourselves is even more difficult than forgiving others. Often times we don't remember why we are hanging onto bitter unforgiveness, and generally we can't remember why we aren't forgiving the other person, and/or God. Many times we can't even recall why we are angry.

A simple act of wrong doing can become insurmountable to our psyches, and is an invasive direct attack that sets us forth on a life long journey of unforgiveness. Why our pain and anger? Is there any way we can get our minds around such complicated and dimensional problems? Transgressions, hurts, resentment, and anger build up in our minds and hearts to the point of no return. Often times it takes a lifetime of sorting through, and a deliberate desire to forgive.

Learning Self-Control

Janice: When our emotions are out of control, we're out of control. Hormones are often blamed for our bad behavior. We blame the weather, our children, and even our spouses, but ultimately we are the ones who are responsible for our misbehavior. Learning self-control can be very challenging from the viewpoint of someone emotionally wounded. Many of you will not want to place the blame on yourself, but will look for a scapegoat. I know how difficult it is to take a look at ourselves, but honesty is necessary if we expect to overcome the obstacles in our lives. I'm not saying it will be smooth sailing and there won't be troubled waters ahead, but the end result will be worth what it takes to get us there. Oh, the joy of a happy and rewarding life can be ours if we're willing to inspect and make the changes necessary for our own emotional and spiritual health.

Bitterness and angry feelings associated with abuse also require a cast-iron determination to overcome. Our emotions have a tendency to override right choices when faced with bad feelings linked to a painful memory. Just how do we accomplish such a feat when we're dragging around a lifetime of emotional baggage? How do we take years of emotional pain and erase its effects? For years, the mere mention of my father pulled from the depths of my soul ugly feelings of bitterness and hatred. The sensation of raw emotional pain would wash over me like a wave crashing on seashore, leaving me crying, bitter, angry, and emotionally spent from the rage inside of me. There were times the pain was so intense all I wanted to do was run and hide, but I had nowhere to go. I was screaming from internal pain like a patient suffering with a ruptured spleen. I truly was sick.

In the midst of the pain, I was forced to look at myself, and the effect rejection and abandonment were having on me. I didn't like what I was seeing, and I knew changes had to come if I was going to live any kind of normal life. I had always believed he deserved to suffer which only stood to justify my own sin of anger. But now I was seeing how those beliefs were robbing me of my joy. Not only was I was emotionally exhausted, I was tired of being trapped by sin. Admitting I felt hatred for him made me realize just how desperately I needed God. When I finally turned my heart and life to Jesus Christ, I began to experience the freedom of real joy and happiness, and I haven't been the same since.

Deb: Lord, I believe I have met my twin in Janice! I close my eyes and hear myself, sharing my life-long thoughts. I believe having come to know you these past nine months has made me feel understood. God had a purpose that day.

Janice: Jesus said, "If ye forgive men their trespasses, your heavenly Father will also forgive you: But if you forgive not men their trespasses, neither will your Father forgive your trespasses" (Matthew 6:14-15). Although I had heard this passage most of my life, the act of forgiveness was something entirely different and more difficult in application. Half of me didn't want to forgive, yet the other half wanted to be right with God. I was very torn. Many of you may look at this wrestling with God as comical, but I assure you the wrestling was more with me than with God. I wanted to do what was right, and it soon became clear unforgiveness wasn't an option. I wrestled back and forth because I didn't know if I could do it. In all honesty I didn't want to forgive him. I thought there is no way God could possibly understand, and He's just asking way too much of me. I couldn't wrap my head around it or see the wisdom in it at all.

I complained to myself, "I was the one hurt, not my father."

To me it wasn't that simple. I reasoned that he was a horrible father, so why did he deserve such mercy? The prison wall I had erected around myself was so high I couldn't see it was me who was suffering, not my father. We only hurt ourselves when we hold onto wrongs perpetrated against us. God, in His wisdom, presses us to face our sinful attitudes and behaviors because there is something good He desires to give us. That "good" is His joy and peace, without which our lives are wrecked. Releasing my ugly pent-up emotions were just the beginning of what God had in store for me. I had carried bitterness and pain, holding onto them like a war trophy of all my scars. Now I was choosing to release them into the hands of a loving, merciful God. Little did I know how forgiving my father would change me, and how it was the first step to becoming an emotionally whole individual.

Deb: God is calling all of us to bare our "trash" to Him, and all of our unworthy moments which probably covers most of our lives. We could never work enough to be worthy of His love, compassion, and forgiveness, but we can accept His grace and unconditional love. However, it's more important that we take the opportunity to pass on His love, grace, and mercy to others. Until I started asking and praying for true discernment for my head knowledge and my heart knowledge to come together, I could have never forgiven. It is only by His grace I could forgive my father. It is the same grace and forgiveness that God extends towards me. It's that simple. As children of God, our ultimate treasure is to become as forgiving of others as He is of us.

The Act of Forgiveness

Janice: Forgiveness truly begins in the heart. We all know just how easy it is to justify angry bitter feelings, especially when we have been on the receiving end of abuse. Forgiveness releases us from the prison walls we have built around ourselves, and opens up a dialog between us and God in which we can truly hear His voice. Saying the words "I forgive you," is an act of obedience pleasing to Him. Sometimes our words and feelings don't line up right away, and we feel we haven't forgiven, but making a concerted effort to crucify our flesh daily goes the distance to truly forgiving from our hearts.

If we confess and believe our heart will agree with our words. "A new heart also will I give you, and a new spirit will I put within you: and I will take away the stony heart out of your flesh, and I will give you a heart of flesh" (Ezekiel 36:26). God is saying He will remove our heart of stone (perverseness) and give us a heart that is pliable (fleshly, soft and compliant) to His will. Our hearts house our minds, our will, our understanding, and our emotions. How we feel should never dictate our obedience. We make choices based upon truth and not on flimsy, unpredictable feelings. Working through forgiveness step by step, we release those who willfully and unknowingly hurt us, leaving to God the time and season He chooses to deal with them.

The Root of Depression

I think America has become the most medicated country in the world as evidenced by the number of people on medications today. A quote from the *Healing Talks Nature's Power,* an online website states: "According to Medco Health Solutions Inc., which manages prescription benefits for about 1 in 5 Americans, over half of Americans are prescription-addicted or daily taking prescription medications for chronic health problems."[19] *ABC News World Report* with Diane Sawyer published a report October 19, 2011, about the number of people on antidepressants. ABC is quoted as follows: "According to new survey data from the Centers for Disease Control and Prevention, one in ten Americans older than twelve are now taking antidepressants—a fourfold increase in the prevalence of antidepressant use since the late 1980s."[20] I wonder why so many people are now on antidepressants? Why such a large number of people medicating themselves to cope with life's problems? Is it possible there is a relationship between depression and bitter unforgiveness? I'm prone to say there is because depression is often rooted in anger associated with unresolved issues.

Unforgiveness is overlooked as a cause for depression. We go to the doctor expecting him or her to fix our problems, and come home with a prescription to bury them. Man-made solutions may work temporarily, but depression is a spiritual problem requiring spiritual answers. So if medication isn't the answer, what is? There is a solution, my friend, and that solution isn't the least bit complicated. We tend to complicate things, but God doesn't. Depression has its roots in deep-seated bitterness, unresolved anger, and unforgiveness. You may angrily say, "I don't have bitterness and anger." I challenge you to dig down deep and find what is troubling you, my friend. Many of you pretend your life is completely together, but gnawing at your heart is something you can't bring yourself to face. Deep inside there is a part of you that you've chosen to keep hidden from others and even God. Maybe it's some kind of abuse you've tried for years to forget, and would have been successful at hiding it had this ugly depression problem not come to the surface of your well put-together life.

Jesus said in the Book of John, "The thief comes to steal, kill and destroy: But I have come that you might have life and have it more abundantly" (John 10:10). Medicating with drugs is a temporary fix, and a huge hindrance to uncovering the truth about ourselves. A genuine desire for emotional and spiritual freedom requires a deliberate act on our part to battle against the sins that so easily get us off course. Those willing to press themselves will find peace and unspeakable joy.

Self-Healing Strategies

I've spoken to a lot of people from all walks of life, and I realize many of us battle the same thought patterns stemming from abuse and trauma. It seems to me emotional trauma is very common, and the need for relief compels some to seek answers in the wrong places.

Man-made solutions to heal spiritual problems offer little chance of finding real answers. Therapists and self-help gurus all over the world claim to have knowledge to inner healing yet few people are ever healed. Thousands and thousands of dollars are spent each year in search of emotional health, yet very few, if any, find it. However, there is an answer, and it's much closer than we may think. It's doesn't take a specialist or self-anointed health guru to show us that true inner healing emerges when we confront our own sin of unforgiveness, and laying our past wounds and hurts at the feet of Jesus. You may say, "That just sounds too easy!" Well, it is that simple because there's only One who has all the answers to life's problems, and that person is God Himself, the One who designed and created us in His image.

New Age gurus have answers for the seeker that appear to be very wise, but behind their teachings we find their wisdom to be earthly and sensual, with an air of seduction that draws one into spiritual deception and away from true spiritual freedom. They do not have the answers to emotional healing and they never will. You may be thinking that's a brave statement to make, but I can say with certainty that God is the only one with the power to heal. I know because I have experienced His healing power in my own life. I wouldn't be able to share with you what He has done in me if I didn't have personal intimate knowledge of His grace and mercy. That's why we can't continue down the road of so called self-acclaimed spiritual healers who have no real experience with God. It only frustrates God's will for our lives.

Something else of importance as we discuss this is that self-help gurus charge exorbitant fees in exchange for their ideas and techniques thought to bring inner healing. But counter to their large over reaching fees is Christ, who has already paid the price for our healing through His shed blood on the cross. Healing has already been paid for. All we have to do is ask for His help and He is there; ready and willing to give us what we ask and need. If you're serious about emotional and spiritual healing, I want to challenge you to offer a prayer to God asking for His help. You may be pleasantly surprised at how He answers.

Self-motivation and self-help methods only take us down the road of deception. If we choose man's ideas over God's ways, our emotional and spiritual healing will not only be delayed, but we risk never finding our answers. Looking for man to save us is like two blind men trying to lead one another; neither can see so both fall into the ditch. The only answer is found in a relationship with Jesus Christ and embracing His redemptive work on the cross. Anything outside the cross will leave us disappointed and empty. I believe the only way to have complete inner healing is through the shed blood of Jesus Christ. Anything other than that is nothing more than man trying to save himself.

Total Surrender

Deb: I am telling you the single best thing that Christ ever did for me was to begin concentrating on my heart. On October 2, 2011, I believe that Jesus Christ truly gave me this prayer to intercede for myself. I couldn't believe the healing power of crying out to God the Father for emotional, physical, mental, and spiritual healing. I know it was intercessory prayer and came from Jesus himself. I didn't believe I had any spiritual hang ups so why would I pray that way? I thought I was at the foot of the cross—literally. Furthermore, I wouldn't have considered mental help either because I felt I had a sound mind and was emotionally well. WOW! If you ever pray for that kind of healing, put your seatbelt on because **what a ride it has been**! You see, all these years I prayed and asked Him for physical healing, but never for the healing of my emotional and spiritual pain. Now He is healing my life in this area as well.

Being confident of this very thing, that he which hath begun a good work in you will perform [it] until the day of Jesus Christ. (Philippians 1:6)

Moving Forward

Janice: Realizing we need emotional health is an important first step if we are serious about changing our lives. Acknowledging we have a problem is only half the battle. The other necessary part is coming to God with an open heart and mind to receive what He has for each of us. I have talked about the necessity of forgiveness, and hope I've been successful in helping each of you understand its vital importance for moving forward. Many of you will try to sidestep this part of the process because deep within your heart you believe it isn't necessary for change. Let me say as soberly as I can, any thought resistant to forgiveness will only make the process longer and more painful. So there must come an understanding that forgiveness is at the very core of inner healing and spiritual renewal. Without it we're just spinning our wheels and wasting our time. We know we can't change the past, but we can change our future. Knowing and expecting others will hurt us or let us down prepares us to handle the feelings of unforgiveness, as they are sure to come.

I'm not perfect! I still have moments when I break down and feel a twinge of unforgiveness shoot through me. When this happens it's my opportunity to say, "God, I trust You and I choose to forgive!" My father has never apologized nor do I expect he ever will. He's never remotely admitted he hurt me or my siblings, and I don't believe he's even aware of the pain he has caused any of us. The bitter unforgiveness that once dominated my life doesn't affect me the same anymore. I no longer experience the raw emotions I felt earlier because I have so much of God in my life there's no room for those kinds of empty thoughts and feelings anymore. The truth is my father may never change, but I can now say with boldness, "That will not change me." As an act of my will, I choose to walk in forgiveness, which helps me to remain free. The times I do see him, I treat him with love and respect even though I never got that from him. Past hurts no longer weigh me down, and I feel such a freedom inside, a renewed sense of just being. God has given me hope with a confidence that I can face whatever may come. I have been set free. Praise God!

Chapter 9

Amazing Grace

For God so loved the world, that he gave his only begotten
Son, that whosoever believeth in him should not perish, but
have everlasting life. (John 3:16)

Deb: This morning as I write, I am reminded of the lyrics of a
Paul McCartney and the Beatles' song, *Yesterday*. How appropriate
these words feel this morning, not for the intention of their song, but
it reflects the pain of my heart, and the gift of His **amazing grace.**

Yesterday, all my troubles seemed so far away
Now it looks as though they're here to stay
Oh, I believe in yesterday
Suddenly I am not half the "woman" I used to be
There's a shadow hanging over me
Oh, yesterday came suddenly.

Beatles. "Yesterday" (Yesterday and Today Album). Capitol Records, 1966.

Somewhere along the way I knew this day would come, but I never realized that fifty years later I would feel the same embarrassment. Because you see, facing it changes everything. Who I thought I was, who I am, and the very fiber of my existence has been "messed with"! Now we can't have a poor pitiful Pearl party, but we can examine the feelings and put them in proper perspective.

Yesterday, all my troubles seemed so far away as I forged ahead with parts of me shutting down completely for what seemed to be eternity. However, the God I serve is so much bigger than that. Here is my take on my life: Jesus shielded me, protected me, encouraged me, and carried me all the while holding me in the palm of His nail scarred hand. I smile and realize how He carries us, imagining the poem, *Footprints in the Sand*. Not only did He get me ready for what was coming, He prepared those around me because my God knew I would need their help.

I have quoted Paul Young, the author of *The Shack*, before and will probably always associate him with, "God is in the details folks!"[21] He's in every detail of my life and your life. I was walking with my husband the other morning when he revealed to me what God was doing in his life. As he witnessed to me, I had goose bumps you could hang your hat on.

Don said, "Deb, God is in the details. Paul is right! If this pain and trauma had been revealed to you five years ago, I may not have been man enough to understand and support you; ten years ago I wouldn't have been man enough. Deb, think of His timing, doesn't it excite you?"

Yes! It does encourage me, so much that I can hardly speak much less write from the cockles of my soul. At this very moment I realize that God heard my prayer when I prayed so many years ago for a husband who would love not only me, but love and honor God foremost. WOW! Did I win the husband lottery or what?

The time line for mercy and grace began as I landed at our beach house in South Carolina the first of June, 2011. I could not physically make it up our steps without a break. I had been to Cleveland Clinic where testing had revealed sixty-five percent blocked carotid arteries bilaterally, along with some problems with my heart due to years of Lupus, high blood pressure, and all the treatments I have withstood over twenty-five years. I was on medications and couldn't tell if it was me or the drugs. Of course, my positive attitude was obviously in denial. I felt miserable and the summer was longer for my family than for me.

In late July, we were sitting quietly on the beach listening to the sounds of the waves rush ashore just in time to chase the seagulls, and the small children further back on the beach.

Don said, "Deb, I think we should consider putting the kids in Christian School down here. You could take it easy until you are back 100 percent, and I could travel back and forth."

I am going to stop here with the argument that took place because I elaborated earlier on this elsewhere in the book. However, I will

tell you in the time line of **grace and mercy** that this was an important event. Yes, me listening to my husband and trusting both he and
God at the same time, was important. You see, up to this point in
my life, I was one of those Christians who believed certain parts of
the Bible and living by them, while I ignored the parts that didn't fit
into my life style. Yes, I am referring to the passage of scripture that
reads, "Men are the head of their families" (see Ephesians 5:22-24).
Whew! I had fought this whole idea of men being the head of their
homes for so long, but strangely God's timing has been perfect in
working out the sinful parts of my carnal nature. I had taken control,
feeling I had to be stronger than I needed to be, and yet wanting my
husband to "Lead For God's Sake,"[22] to quote my dear sweet friend,
Todd Gongwer, author of you guessed it, *LEAD FOR GOD'S SAKE*!

Bottom line is we stayed. The kids were happy, and for the first
time in my life, I was not afraid of being alone. I was, however, so
miserable in the solitude of my wilderness that I began to cry out to
God. To make myself feel better, I would pick up the phone to try
and offer my involvement or help, always with someone I didn't
know well, since I was new to the full-time life on Hilton Head. All
of this was an effort to bring myself out of loneliness. I had spent the
biggest part of my life busying myself helping and serving others,
but suddenly I found myself in a place where no one knew who or
whose I was. I was the new kid on the block.

I'll admit the struggle was so hard I talked to myself saying,
"Don't they know I am a woman of my own dreams if nothing else?

Don't they realize I am here to help?" The ministers I called seemed shocked that I would say, "Here I am, use me." I thought maybe they don't know Chip Ingram's philosophy, "The Church of today needs ministers in every pew." You need to go to the pastor of your church and say, "I have these strengths, and I want to do whatever." Be involved! If you haven't attended one of Chip's home studies, I suggest you do so, especially the Miracle of Life Change. Oh, how God transforms His children! At any rate, I felt rejected, odd, and certainly out of place. However, God had a plan of healing and He needed Deb alone and broken.

You know in my home town of Charleston, WV, there are not many ministers who would be shocked to receive a phone call from me informing them of an event I was pulling together in which I needed their help. I would call Barry Moll, Matt Santen, Monty Brown, Father Sadie, and Rabi Ureci anytime and they would smile and say, "It's you again!" The late Reverend David Jasper was another I knew I could always call and ask for his involvement. He would gladly call others and have them at the meeting on my behalf.

Oh, how I miss Pastor David's faith. He was always so willing and supportive of any cause with my name on it because he knew me. His sweet and tender words were left as a memory in the front of a book he bought me just prior to his death, "I look forward to serving with you." The man didn't have a shred of pride or ego, and how inviting and enabling of Him to want to serve with the likes of a person attending his services. WOW! Talk about empowering the congregation. But now I wasn't home, people didn't know me nor had they any idea how much I loved God. I'm sure I came off as weird. I am reminded how we as Christians tend to wait to check out the new people coming in. It is a bit ironic since churches pray and seek God for church growth.

While I am taking a stroll down memory lane, another very inspiring Pastor/mentor to me is Barry Moll. Barry never met a stranger and was always jovial. I believe the Lord filled him up each morning. Some of the most powerful sermons I have ever heard preached were the ones prior to his leaving our church. Before the new pastor arrived, Pastor Moll instructed us through deliberate messages and scripture, to be prayerful for our new minister. He was preparing the congregation to receive our new pastor, much like God prepares us long before He steps in. He further asked us to pray that the congregation would accept and love him, learning all that we could from him during his appointed time with us. Yes, Barry, that was taken from my journal. You said it brother. His divinely appointed time with us offered so much because Barry Moll did his work without pride or ambition for himself. His interest for God and the building of His kingdom were genuine. Oh, praise God that through the years I have sat in the church pews where God placed me.

Now let's get back to the rest of my story. Imagine me, a woman who had been in business most of her life, owning businesses of 4000 employees, and traveling across the United States teaching His Word, finding herself standing face-to-face with God. I was used to speaking to large audiences of people because they were hungry for *Attitude Therapy*. However, I left those meetings knowing in the depths of my soul that there was more to the story. Every time I preached *Attitude Therapy,* God would place a person in the audience who would ask, "Are you a Christian?" I would proudly respond, "Yes!" Then they would inform me that I should be working full time in the ministry. Instantly my smile would become plastic and guilt ridden. It wasn't until I was fifty years old that I decided to work full-time for Him!

Now back to the story of healing. Before I was fully recovered, I hit the ground running! Calling every pastor I remotely knew or had attended a service at their church. I was interviewing, I think or maybe I was testing the waters. We were looking for a place to plug in, and I was open to God's direction and instruction. I was very bold in asking some of these pastors to lunch, forgetting I was in the South and women don't do that sort of thing. Basically, I was clueless and it didn't matter if they knew me or not, didn't they know I worked full-time for God? It's possible I may have even come off as bold a few times. I was like a "fireball" just wanting to be used. I had forgotten God wanted this to be a time of healing and looking inwardly.

Realizing what I was doing, I humbly prostrated myself before Him and said, "I am sorry, once again, Father. I got on a 'roll' without You, Lord Jesus, doing what Deb thought was right."

You see we can even get pushy doing His work. I believe my troubles are being reconciled. I am showing grace and that is when forgiveness takes place. An author friend of mine was on the island for a visit recently, so we put together a nice dinner party for him and his family.

As everyone was leaving, a pastor thanked us and said, "What did I do to deserve such a wonderful meal and an evening like this?"

I said, "God told me to invite you and your family."

I believe people expect you to either want something for your "works" or they try to figure out why me? I am tuned in to Jesus Christ because I am in the business of doing just what He says.

A few years ago I launched this campaign within my family: If God says, "Turn left at the stop light," even if I'm running frantically late for car pool, I am turning left. I am going where He leads me. I have the determination to put Him above the kids, plans, life, tennis lessons, or whatever has brought me to this point of redemption in my life. The journey of healing takes place step by step and process by process. My heart says; "In His sweet time, not Deb's time."

The next line of the song is, "I believe in yesterday." Well, I do when you think of the multitude of baby steps it has taken to get me here. But more importantly I believe in a risen Savior who is in this world today. I believe I am standing on Holy Ground when I enter the gates of thanksgiving in my morning time with Him. I purpose-fully humble myself and come to Him with praise, thanksgiving, and believing that all things work together for them who love Him. I have a sound knowledge that resonates in my soul because of my yesterdays. I know He is the Great Physician, the Healer of my heart, the Beginning and the Ending. Had it not been for my journey, I could not stand up and say I am planted like a tree by the river of living waters, and I shall not be moved. If Satan uses temptations to make me sin, the Lord Jesus will help me to stand firmly planted in Him. If it wasn't for the beauty of learning forgiveness, I couldn't show grace to others. Grace is forgiveness times ten. I feel my heart and head are now connected as one.

Suddenly, I am not half the woman I used to be. Praise Him for all eternity; I am not half the woman of my dreams, but becoming the woman of His dreams. I learned that phrase from my son, Matt, who lives in Denver, Colorado, much too far away from his momma. Hint! Hint! He used to call out to God, "Make me the man of Your dreams!" I love it! That is really what life is all about and I learned it from my kid! WOW! See Matthew, I was listening. I am not half the woman, but growing into the one who can represent Him better. More worthy each day of offering Him to the many women and children I minister to regularly. Finally, "the shadow hanging over me" became my wall of protection for me. If you don't let people in, they can't hurt you. I am gladly celebrating the shadow which hung over me because I wouldn't have been in the scriptures hunting for the Master. James 1:25 speaks of the man who looks intently into the "perfect law of liberty." If I had not known rejection and betrayal maybe I wouldn't have needed answers. I am forgiven because I sought the scripture; I am redeemed because I trusted Him. I know grace and pardon because of His redemption. "My chains are gone

I have been set free," Chris Tomlin sings with such unfeigned love for God. I have unending mercy and amazing grace. Chris Tomlin perhaps says it all in the lyrics from *"You Are My King"*

"You Are My King"

I'm forgiven because you were forsaken

I'm accepted, you were condemned

I'm alive and well

Your Spirit is within me

Because you died and rose again

I'm forgiven because you were forsaken

I'm accepted, you were condemned

I'm alive and well

Your Spirit is within me

Because you died and rose again

Amazing love how can it be?

That you my King would die for me

Amazing love, I know it's true

It's my joy to honor you

Amazing love how can it be?

That you my King would die for me

Amazing love, I know it's true

It's my joy to honor you

In all I do

I honor you

Tomlin, Chris. "You Are My King" (Amazing Love Album).Sparrow Records, 2000.

Janice, I know that it is your desire, too. To honor Him as it is mine and I believe that as Chris Tomlin continues to sing praises to The Almighty God, others will hear the call as well. Here is a cute story I read on grace by Bob Deffinbaugh.

I have a friend whose experience gives us some insight into the doctrine of the grace of God. He had just returned from Viet Nam where he had served in the Army. Upon his release he had insufficient funds to fulfill a longtime desire to own a new Jaguar. Early one morning he was driving in a remotely populated part of Oklahoma which, he reasoned, was the perfect place to find out how fast the car would go. The speedometer was easing its way past 160 as the powerful sports car reached the top of a small rise. Just beyond, a highway patrolman was waiting. A law-abiding citizen, my friend slammed on the brakes, slid past the officer at 150 miles per hour, and came to a halt some distance down the road.

Before long, the officer caught up and stood beside the sleek convertible.

"Do you have any idea how fast you were going?" he inquired.

"Well roughly," was the deliberately evasive reply.

"One hundred sixty-three miles per hour!" the officer specified.

"That's about what I thought," my friend confessed, somewhat sheepishly.

Guilt was obvious, and there was no possible excuse to be offered. My friend could only wait to discover what this fiasco was going to cost. He meekly waited for the officer to proceed.

To his amazement the patrolman queried, "Would you mind if I took a look at that engine?"

The fine points of high performance automobiles cannot be discussed quickly, so both went on to a coffee shop where they could talk further. A while later, both of the men shook hands and went their separate ways. My friend was elated, for the officer had not given him a citation.

That is about as close to grace as one can come on this earth, but it is still not quite up to the standard of biblical grace. (I say that because biblical grace would be demonstrated only if the patrolman had paid for the coffee.)The principle of grace is as fundamental to Christianity as that of justice is to Law, or love is to marriage. Christianity cannot be understood apart from an adequate grasp of grace. The doctrine of grace distinguishes the Christian faith from every other religion in the world, as well as from the cults. Rightly understood and applied, the doctrine of grace can revolutionize one's Christian life.[23]

Janice: That was truly an awesome example of God's grace and so funny!

Deb: Janice, as I pondered grace the following quote came to mind:

All the joy the world contains
Has come through wishing happiness for others.
All the misery the world contains
Has come through wanting pleasure for oneself.
(Shanti deva)

As I continued to ponder grace, I thought grace is somewhat like that beautiful quote above. I believe the grace the world contains is from the good deeds God calls His people to do by filling the painful areas of others less fortunate. A lot of the misery people experience comes from holding God off at an arm's length instead of being open to His call upon us to share grace and joy in this world as His workers.

Grace is therefore, God's unmerited favor—His goodness towards those who have no claim on grace, or a reason to expect divine intervention or favor. The principle manifestation of God's grace has been in the form of a gift, and often times this gift is from a "God thing." How many times do we meet someone who had just the right answer to our dilemma and say, "Oh! Now that's a God thing?" And it is! We are the mouthpiece, arms, and legs for God.

That is why if we have a proud heart, or an exterior which cannot be penetrated by God, we are useless to the building of His kingdom. To be someone's grace today should be our individual goal by putting off the prideful things in our carnal nature, and delving into the business of God the Father. Always remember, "God resists the proud, but gives grace to the humble" (1 Peter 5:5).

As I further pondered grace, I thought of two animals joined together with a yoke so that they stay in the right direction, pulling together to achieve the ultimate goal. Christ is so awesome that He would be yoked with me. That He would not only be yoked with me to support and help me work toward my ultimate home, but that He does carry the load, and far more that I can even dream of doing. What a team my God and me! He shows so much grace in this visual. Through Him, we have the energy to go out and show His grace for another by helping them, without any desire for payback. This illustration shows me how much further I have to work on being more Christ like.

Janice, I can see me yoked with you and how our Master has ordained this project. What a God moment we just had! You called to encourage me out of the blue. The words you spoke to me were of God. First, you had no idea I was having a hard day. Secondly, I pray each morning to see God in others and for someone to see God in me. I just saw God in you when you called and told me you understand how difficult my writing about the past can be. We immediately praised Him for His work and anointing upon this gift from the heart. Your words were kind and generous to my soul. Why don't you repeat them as I loved hearing them, and I think our readers would love to be uplifted as you have uplifted me?

Janice: Oh my dear sister, I see that God has tenderly and lovingly brought you to this moment. He knew you would arrive here one day, and He so patiently prepared your heart to receive the healing He knew you needed all along. He is such a wonderful Father, never putting more on us than we are able to bear. Throughout the years He has tenderly pruned and removed the dead places from your heart in order that you may receive the gift He wanted to give you all along. That gift, my friend, is the gift of healing for both your heart and mind. Your healing has given way to an emotional freedom you have only dreamed of. Walking this way means being free from fear, free from the past, and a freedom to be who God called you to be in the beginning. His call is that we become vessels fit for His use, vessels of honor and not dishonor.

We honor God when we humbly receive His loving correction, allowing Him to work unhindered in our lives, weeding and pulling out hurts that limit us in our ability to hear and know Him. That is what He desires—to use us to help others, to encourage and uplift during their time of need. If we had never suffered, we wouldn't be where we are at this moment of letting others know we understand because we have walked in their shoes. We've come out on the other side because of His grace (unmerited favor) and mercy has carried us through.

I've said many times before and I will say it again, "If I could go back to the beginning of my life knowing what I know now, I wouldn't change a thing."

Those are pretty powerful words coming from someone whose life almost ended before it even began. It is, but I would not be the person I am today had I not suffered. I wouldn't be able to stand in the shoes of another and understand the depth of their pain or sorrow had I not suffered. I wouldn't be able to effectively pray God's healing power, and experience His saving grace had I not suffered. I'm so thankful that God trusted me to suffer!

Deb: Janice, have you ever been so thirsty that you felt dehydrated? You pop the lid off a water bottle, toss your head back, and feel the water begin to quench your thirst. I ask you, "Is there a better feeling than those parched lips being satisfied?" Sometimes you feel your heart racing to keep up with the gulps, and other times you stand amazed at how thirsty you must have been to consume a whole bottle of water. My mind then goes to those who do not have the luxury of water. My heart breaks.

The same is true with our faith and the delivery of grace. I am astounded to know that there are those in the church who do not know Him personally, and who do not take a regular prayer time with Him daily. It never ceases to amaze me that those who are believers don't put in the time. There is no better reward than the grace our loving Savior has to offer. It fills us up and quenches our soul. I can't believe people don't come to this healing fountain. I think of hungering and thirsting for His amazing grace. The old hymn, *He Giveth More Grace,* says, "He giveth more grace when our burdens grow greater. He sendeth more strength when our labors increase." I believe it, Janice. I'm living proof.

One of my favorite scriptures down through the years has been, "Be careful for nothing; but in everything by prayer and supplication with thanksgiving let your requests be made known unto God" (Philippians 4:6). I believe it was always one of my favorites growing up because of its reference of worry. My kids will tell you that when they come to me troubled, the same advice is given to them. It may be because it literally applies to every situation and every desire or worry of the heart.

I say, "Do not worry about anything, but pray about everything."

Isn't that powerful? It basically says what I have been so guilty of all these years. Isn't it odd that my favorite scripture is one that I have had the most trouble with in retrospect? Basically, stop worrying and trying to figure it out. Rest in Him, for He is the one who knows the conclusion.

Absolutely! He knows the plan and designed us to live counting on Him to have full knowledge of what we need. He wants our hearts open to Him as we trust Him with everything. WOW! What trust that takes, but oh, how it pays off in **grace**, a grace that is sufficient for our souls. Remember the words to the old hymn? "Grace, Grace, God's Grace. Grace that can pardon and cleanse within." I need a cleansing each day to get the earthly living out and make room for my spiritual Master to fill me up with His grace. Janice, if I were to ask you why is God's grace so amazing, what would you say?

Janice: Deb, I would be tempted to just quote the stanza of *Amazing Grace*. "I once was lost, but now I'm found." Unfortunately, many of us are still lost searching for approval and acceptance in the wrong places. The place in which we receive full assurance of grace is in the arms of our Savior Jesus Christ. It is only through His kindness and generosity that our sins and failures are pardoned, granting us exemption from our wrongs.

Deb: Yes, and as I explained to a lady at lunch today, God is always there. It is us who moves by becoming preoccupied with our own self-sufficiency. God stands still. It is us who orbit around Him. Sometimes we check in with Him, and other times we believe we are doing fine on our own. I was a horrible daughter-in-law. I did not have parents who were in my life so I didn't have experience. My mom had passed and my dad was uninvolved. Many times in my life I don't think to call my in-laws on Sundays and check in. Now that my children have grown, I would be so sad if they didn't check in. Think how God's heart is broken by our independence.

Janice: "I was blind, but now I see," sums it all up I think. God has the uncanny ability to remove our spiritual blindness, letting us see His amazing grace at work in our lives. I've known you a short time, but God's amazing grace is clearly evident in your life as He is continuing to bring emotional healing. I love listening to you tell of His goodness every time we talk.

Deb: Well Janice, as you know I love to tell about it because it is bragging on our awesome Father, the Great Healer. He has delivered me many times from health issues and brought me out of the depths of darkness. It is easy to say that casually, but boy when you are down in the valley, begging for help, it is something to literally shout about. His redemption and His amazing grace is what carry us through so much. I know, my sweet sister, He has done that and more for you, too, which reminds me of the ending of *Amazing Grace* which says, "the hour I first believed." He has stood with me on the mountain tops and in the valleys. In the good and in the bad He has carried me. He has sustained me even when the love of a husband or child could not.

Janice: In the country of Switzerland is a little town called "Binn." This small town is just like any other small town except for the fact it has something that most people aren't aware is even there. Deep in the lush valley are laid very rich mineral deposits, some of which are very unique. To quote Wikipedia, "It is noted among the mineralogical community for its unusual sulfosalt specimens."[24] You may be wondering what does this have to do with suffering. Let me explain. Much like the unique treasures found in the valley of Binn, deep in the dark valleys of our lives are the "rich treasures" of the soul. This is the place God takes the broken things in our lives, and turns them into treasures to be used for His kingdom. Life's twists and turns seemingly have a direction all their own, and life has a way of presenting challenges in areas we need the most improvement. Often the challenges we face come through suffering, hardship, and pain. We cringe at the very notion of suffering, running from the very idea that it can help us in some way.

But just consider for a moment that we lived in a world where every day we were perched on the highest mountain top. What if our well thought out plans went just the way we imagined they would? What if we never experienced trouble or disappointment of any kind? What kind of person do you think you would be? Would you be a better person or would you become someone who was the center of their own world? What do you think your life would look like? Let me suggest to you that we would be stagnant and stop growing altogether. We would be the self-centered, self-seeking person down the street that we don't like, because we would have little if any regard for our neighbor, our friend, our colleague, or our brother. In the valley experience are life's many lessons which offer a multitude of treasures to be discovered. In the dark valley of our lives we discover compassion, kindness, understanding, long-suffering, patience, meekness, and many more things that make us better people. "But the fruit of the Spirit is love, joy, peace, longsuffering, gentleness, goodness, faith, Meekness, temperance: against such there is no law" (Galatians 5:22-23).

Our fleshly natures which consist of our carnal thoughts, out of control emotions, insatiable wants, and inordinate desires, are destroyed in the valley experience. This often comes with great pain. It's through our hardship that we learn obedience, letting go of our carnal nature and learning to embrace God's redeeming truth. "Though he were a Son, yet learned he obedience by the things which he suffered" (Hebrews 5:8). The valley has a way of softening us so that God can bring His love and correction to our lives. I believe suffering is one of the catalysts the Lord uses to mold and shape us into His image. Suffering strips away our façade and reveals the "Pearl of Great Price" we are underneath.

Chapter 10

Unending Love

Seeing ye have purified your souls in obeying the truth through the Spirit unto unfeigned love of the brethren, [see that ye] love one another with a pure heart fervently. (1 Peter 1:22)

Deb: How great is the love that our God has lavished upon us? I want to bathe in it—soak in it—let it seep into the very pores of my being every morning. Then, and only then, will I be equipped to even begin to think about **love.**

"Our Father, I open myself to Your love, and commit myself as a vessel to be used by You. I have no idea what I will be like as life goes on any more than I can hardly recall what I was like as a child. But I fully trust You and give 100% of me to You and offer myself as Your disciple."

Janice: Deb, you and I are singing the same song of praise. I wipe the tears as I contemplate the unity of our hearts as we desire to serve Him through collectively writing this book. To God be all the glory for the wondrous love He has shown to us both.

Deb: Jesus tells us in His Word about **love.**

"You have heard that it was said, 'Love your neighbor and hate your enemy'. But I tell you: 'Love your enemies and pray for those who persecute you, that you may be sons of your Father in heaven.' He causes his sun to rise on the evil and the good, and sends rain on the righteous and the unrighteous. If you love those who love you, what reward will you get? Are not even the tax collectors doing that? And if you greet only your brothers, what are you doing more than others? Do not even pagans do that? Be perfect, therefore, as your heavenly Father is perfect." (Matthew 5:43-48 NIV)

Janice: Deb, I just love that scripture and how Jesus points out the importance of loving in our everyday lives. It's easy to love only those who love us back, but loving our enemies proves we belong to God. Christ set the example of loving His enemies, even those who hung Him on the cross. They killed Him, yet He loved them. How many of us are willing to help someone we consider to be against us? I dare say most of us would think nothing of passing them by if they asked for our help. This passage of scripture is just as important to us today as it was back then. If we desire to be like Christ, we must **love** like Christ and that means loving our enemies.

Deb: I must admit that this is a tall order. Janice, I love Jesus, but love my neighbors, does that mean me? Even when they aren't nice or I become aggravated with their children? Jesus' love is so predictable and all encompassing. Mine on the other hand is rather lame. I think about the times a man has sat too close on the airplane, perhaps leaned over a little too far on my side of the chair. How I wanted to take my hand and put it down his throat, pull his heart out, and shred it. Can you imagine saying that you love Jesus, yet wrestling with those kinds of thoughts? To love as Jesus can be staggering. I am trying to live up to that kind of challenge, and ultimately with His help I will, but it is overwhelming at best when you think of how far beneath the bar we end up falling. *Help me, Father God, to love as You do.*

Janice: Deb, we all battle with these same kinds of thoughts that don't reveal God's love in our hearts. All of mankind is born of the flesh and act out in the flesh, yet through salvation we are now born of the Spirit, taking on the very nature of Christ. It takes the Holy Spirit to come in and change the way we think and feel, putting on Christ's love, and loving those we think don't deserve it. I can understand the world not loving the unlovely, but Christians should set the moral standard of what it means to love the unlovely. We should be the example of Christ's love to the world.

Deb: I know that there is no randomness about my life or its direction. I wake up afresh to each new dawn that God loaned me, every precious day, with the question to our Savior, "What will

You have me do with it?" Janice, I don't want my daily breathes or minutes to pass through my fingers like sand. I want to experience the newness of God's gifts, "partake in the here and now and just love on everybody." I rejoice that He loves me so, and I want to pay it forward, if you will.

Janice: Deb, I do cherish every day the Lord gives me, and, like you, I want my life to count for something. I agree we need to step back taking in this gift we call life, and live it for His Glory and benefit. Christ came as a servant, therefore we should be servants one to another. The mentality of most people is that of being served by others, but in all truth, to be like Christ means to devote ourselves to the interests of someone else. I think that is why you and I have connected on the spiritual level. We both desire to serve God with all of our hearts, allowing Him to use us, giving hope to others, and building up His kingdom here on earth.

Deb: I want to intimately connect my heart with our Lord of lords. It allows me no time for planning, worrying, fixing, controlling, or feeling the need to be in charge. You see, I believe we wake up and go after it in the flesh, allowing our carnal appetites to take over. We must ask the precious Redeemer of our souls to point us in the right direction, and place our feet upon the path that He prepared for our day, map questing, if you will, our journey. Yesterday, while mailing out some books at the post office, a lady with a walker approached the counter. I witnessed the love and compassion of the postal employee as he was obviously familiar with the dear client. As she left I stopped addressing my overnight packages and stepped over to open the door to assist her. She smiled, and her ocean blue eyes twinkled as a tear ran down her precious, tan mature cheek. As we bided each other ado, I went back to my rushing and panic filled afternoon.

As I left, I noticed that it had taken her literally eighteen minutes to walk to her car, put away her walker, and make her way to the driver's side of the car. I approached her and we shared conversations about our lives. I noticed that time was once again calling, as it was soon time to pick up the children from school. I made a conscious effort to ignore the time constraints of my earthly life, and to purposefully stay focused on this dear sister. Story after story, chapter after chapter of life's disappointments rolled off her tongue with little time for input or interruption. I listened, smiled, nodded, and offered my Jesus as a refuge. I pray that He once again calls her name this week and that she fondly answers.

Janice: Deb, you are right! We are often so caught up with "to do lists" that we fail to see the person next to us. I'm so glad you took the time to share with this dear woman the love of God. We never know who God will send our way so it's important that we be ready to, "Preach the Word; be prepared in season and out of season; correct, rebuke and encourage—with great patience and careful instruction" (2 Timothy 4:2 NIV).

Deb: Life is made up of these opportunities and these precious moments where we can simply offer love, His magnificent love. She asked me why I had been so patient and willing to listen. I admitted that listening is not one of my strengths, talking is, and interrupting is a sin I constantly fight. I told her that God and I had been talking, and that He had called me out on my earthly personality that is constantly rushed, crazed, dazed, and confused. He had mentioned to me that I should be calm, relaxed, ever present, and ready to listen by showing His love to others. Not only did my taking time to show love help her, but I was blessed immensely. So I suppose He helped me be the neighbor that I am called to be right there in the post office parking lot.

Janice: What a beautiful testimony, and one I know you won't soon forget nor will she. God is amazing, and if we will only listen, He can direct our paths exactly where we need to go. Loving others isn't just talking about what God has done for us, but it is showing them what God can do for them. It may mean helping our next door neighbor change the tire on their car, or feeding a homeless person on the street. Whatever it is, let Christ love through you, and you will be amazed how God will come in, changing our times and circumstances.

For I was a hungered, and ye gave me meat: I was thirsty, and ye gave me drink: I was a stranger, and ye took me in: Naked, and ye clothed me: I was sick, and ye visited me: I was in prison, and ye came unto me. (Matthew 25: 35-36)

And the King shall answer and say unto them, Verily I say unto you, Inasmuch as ye have done [it] unto one of the least of these my brethren, ye have done [it] unto me. (Matthew 25:40)

To give light to them that sit in darkness and [in] the shadow

of death, to guide our feet into the way of peace. (Luke 1:79)

Deb: You know, Janice, I want that peace that flows like a river into my soul. I believe it comes from showing love and walking in the path He has for each of us. I truly pray my children, grandchildren, and my husband walk this path of peace and transparency in Christ Jesus. And I pray the same for you and your family.

Janice: Jesus said that if we so much as give a drink of water to what is considered the least in this world, it is as if we did it unto Him. That's why it's so important to not overlook the man or woman on the street wearing dirty clothes, the alcoholic crying out for help, the prisoner behind prison walls, or the drug addicted teenager who has run away from home with nowhere to turn. They may be considered the least in this world, but Christ accounts them as someone He dearly loves. And if He loves them, then we should love them by being His children, emulating His words and actions. Most of us want to pass over these scriptures because we are uncomfortable reaching out to the stained and unlovely of this world. We give with condition, making excuses for not giving to the helpless and down cast because the good we do for them may be used wrongly.

"But love ye your enemies, and do good, and lend, hoping for nothing again; and your reward shall be great, and ye shall be the children of the Highest: for he is kind unto the unthankful and [to] the evil" (Luke 6:35). Why do we sit in the seat of judgment thinking we can determine who receives and who doesn't? It is our responsibility to love at all times, showing forth the grace and mercy of the Father, no matter who they are or where they come from.

Deb: Another great scripture is, "No man can serve two masters: for either he will hate the one, and love the other; or else he will hold to the one, and despise the other. Ye cannot serve God and mammon. Therefore I say unto you, Take no thought for your life, what ye shall eat, or what ye shall drink; nor yet for your body, what ye shall put on. Is not the life more than meat, and the body than raiment?" (Matthew 6:24-25). We expectantly gaze heavenly realizing that God takes care of the birds and the flowers. They long for nothing. Everything they need He provides. And of course the same is true for us. Oh, how He loves you and me. I have everything I need and more abundantly, as do so many of us.

"God, we just want to stop and say thank You and sing praises to You and express our gratitude. We are so fortunate. Thank You doesn't seem strong enough in that we are truly amazed at Christ Jesus love for us."

In carpool I was telling my children this morning about learning to take time to appreciate God's love. There are many people who end up in a hospital bed or a prison only to discover their timeout has led them to knowing Christ in a more real and magnificent way. I told them that I had come to depend on God more deeply than ever before. I explained this past year that dad's travelling overnight has caused me to read more in the Word about the intentional path He has for my life.

I gave the example with dad being gone this morning, and how I will spend two hours with God, praying over our family, and allowing Him to talk to me. Some mornings are cut short because I want to be with my husband, so I hurry through my morning ritual or delay it until the afternoon. I explained to them that being without daddy is like being in a prison. During the time he is gone, I use my wilderness to grow in Christ. They liked the example, and, at thirteen years old I feel they "get it." I believe Jesus is impacting their lives in this extra time I have with them. I can easily feel guilty of working too much when the older children were younger. I quickly ask God for forgiveness, and ask that He take that energy to a good place of doing more for Him. Otherwise, I could get into a sad place of unforgiveness for myself.

Janice: Like you, Deb, many times I still struggle with forgiving myself, beating myself up for not doing the things I know to be right. Sometimes I fail to love myself allowing anger and sadness to control me. I especially struggle when it comes to my children for I know I only have a short while before they are grown and gone. But then I am reminded of His great love for me, and I am able to get to that place of love and forgiveness. "And it shall come to pass, if ye shall hearken diligently unto my commandments which I command you this day, to love the LORD your God, and to serve him with all your heart and with all your soul" (Deuteronomy 11:13).

Deb: You have heard me refer to October 2, 2011, the day that I became totally honest with the Lord Jesus Christ, trusting Him with my entire being. I have a love affair with Christ, and I know that He is the healer of my soul. I pray that He will continue this healing in both of us. There is a sweet anointing upon us to share this with our audience. Someone will be helped today because we have laid our burdens at His feet and admitted unforgiveness of ourselves and others. I feel the divine Holy Spirit's presence and know these heavy burdens will be lifted from us and our readers as they read and pray.

Love heals all! I have love written on a small scripture board in my kitchen this week. Love does cure all!

If we love:

We see things differently

- We listen to one another deliberately and on purpose
- We respect others perspective
- Communicate more clearly as we love each other
- Place importance on the feelings of others
- We play fair
- We are more deliberate in our acts of kindness and expect nothing in return

And now abideth faith, hope, charity, these three; but the greatest of these [is] charity. (1 Corinthians 13:13)

Love is something I do well, but haven't always accepted from others well. I may gloss over not letting the actions of others penetrate me. I may not accept love well because of my own childhood fears and painful memories, or I may be a giver, not a taker because I thought I could control me and the actions of others. But you see, I can't control others and how they choose to give their love. Complicated? A bit, especially when we feel we must control everything. It is much simpler when we fit into His plan of mercy and grace, trusting His will for us. The same is true with love. Our calling is to put it out there and let the world receive it.

Janice: I completely agree. Many will argue it's hard to put ourselves out there when people aren't receptive. But Jesus put Himself out there knowing He would be rejected. The difference is that He gave them the choice to receive or reject His love. On the other hand we become offended when we aren't received with open arms. We certainly can't force others to receive what we offer, but we can love them anyway when they reject and refuse what we desire to give.

Deb: Yesterday evening, as my two youngest children and I landed at the airport, my husband who loves and receives love freely, was there at the airport with a sign, "Pick up for LUCCI Family," with a rose in one hand for me, and two chocolate suckers for each of the kids, in the other. We laughed and people shared in our joy.

One lady said to Don, "You are so sweet!"

Another watched with tears in her eyes, and I wondered what she was thinking. Did she have that longing to be loved by her husband or loved one, who would do something so gracious, or perhaps in earlier years had, but he was gone, or was she just feeling the love for us? Now keep in mind we had been away from each other two and half days, not two and half weeks. It was so awesome with as much as we all travel, that he would take the time and energy to get out of the car and come into the airport to wait. That he would plan ahead to buy a rose and chocolate suckers from their favorite spot, and then make a childish sign with his own hands, and be man enough to stand in public with all his love and affection, is awesome! The first time I picked him up at an airport he had a dozen roses for me. Let me tell you that will keep a girl coming back. Now you see why I married him! I am one smart and lucky gal. Although what he did was a simple act of kindness, his actions truly were a reflection of God Himself.

Each day I pray, "Let me see God in others and let others see God in me." A friend of mine said this one day in prayer, and I immediately added it to my tool box of prayers and devotion, "It means so much to me." It is a great way to set up the day for Holy Spirit encounters; an invitation for good, if you will. Talk about attitude adjustments, try praying that way and see what happens. My eyes are wide open as I look for God daily as a confirmation through what people say or do. Think of the gifts that simple prayers add because I am aware. It's a great measuring device for me in case I become less than patient, and, quite frankly, it holds me steady knowing that I have prayed it and others are looking for a glimpse of God in me.

Janice: I just love that story. I can see the anticipation on Don's face as he waits for you and your kids to arrive. How blessed you are to have that kind of love and adoration.

Deb: Love cures so much. It provides the world with happiness. It is such a strong word and such a beautiful expression. Scripture tells us, "God is love" (1 John 4:16). Whoever walks in love lives for God, and God lives in them. My oldest son, Matthew is the most amazing young man. He has "lived" this verse from the time he was a little boy, often seeing it as the most important verse in the Bible. I think of him every time the Lord is working on me and teaching me to love from my spirit. Even if a person isn't spiritual in nature look at Wikipedia, the free online encyclopedia, and see what it says about love. Love is an emotion of strong affection and personal attachment. Love is also a virtue representing all of human kindness, compassion, and affection; the unselfish loyal and benevolent concern for the good of another.

I suppose when you get down to it, the reason we are writing this book is out of our love for Christ. If you will recall, Janice, I said, "No," to this project carnally for months. I said I have no interest in getting busy, proofing at 5:00 a.m. in the morning, having only gone to bed just a few hours earlier. I certainly felt I would never share my experience of this past year. I looked heavenly at one point and said to God, "I will never speak of this again." Out of love and humble obedience, I submit my writing to Him to be used for His glory. I am laying this offering of love at His feet. Because we have been given so much we too must give. "Freely you have received, freely give" (Matthew 10:8).

Janice: Love is a word flippantly tossed around in our society so much that it's meaning is lost in its overuse. We love Italian cuisine, we love our new hairstyle, we love the Green Bay Packers, we love going to the beach, or we love any object we have an extreme admiration for, etc. Our society confuses love with infatuation, a feeling associated with "falling in love." This kind of love lasts for a short while until reality kicks in. This is where the real confusion starts in that those highly intense feelings we felt earlier are now gone, and we believe we've fallen out of love.

But God's definition of love isn't defined so loosely because He is the very essence and epitome of love. Love is the very nature and special quality that He alone expresses to us and through us to others. That's what I mean by the word "essence."

Charity suffers long, [and] is kind; charity envies not; charity vaunts not itself, is not puffed up, Doth not behave itself unseemly, seeks not her own, is not easily provoked, thinks no evil; Rejoices not in iniquity, but rejoices in the truth; Bears all things, believeth all things, hopes all things, endures all things. (1 Corinthians 13:4-7)

There are nine characteristics of divine love which exhibit themselves in patience, kindness, generosity, humility, courtesy, unselfishness, a good temper, righteousness, and sincerity. God exhibits all of these divine qualities because He is one and the same. With all truthfulness, can we say we reflect God's true divine nature to others? I know I fall short of the mark even though I strive to live God's Word every day. "He that loves not knows not God; for God is love" (1 John 4:8). Vine's Expository Dictionary of Old Testament Words says of Christian love, "Is not an impulse from the feelings, it does not always run with the natural inclinations, nor does it spend itself only upon those for whom some affinity is discovered. Love seeks the welfare of all, and works no ill to any; love seeks opportunity to do good to all men, and especially toward them that are of the household of the faith."[25] We cannot claim to know God, if we don't love others. Deb, our love is inspired by God Himself. Our desire is to give to each of you what He has given us, which is His love and acceptance. Like you said earlier, Deb, we are writing this book as an extension of God's undying love and mercy for all, in hopes of turning them to Him with their whole heart, mind, and body.

Deb: Janice, when I think of love, I think of Starbucks. In my opinion people aren't in line for Java, they are in line to be loved on. Have you ever been addressed so generously and so kindly? The employees are excited to "serve" you. I once gave myself a huge lecture. I prompted myself that even though I teach *Attitude Therapy* across the country, I notice when Starbucks and Chick-fil-A do it just right—that I must challenge myself to treat my children as though I was serving them. By the third morning I was back to, "grab the orange juice out of the fridge; we need to get a move on." I know we all can improve on the endeavor to simply love each other. One of my favorite songs I listen to on my morning walks with the dogs is by New Worldson, *Learning to be the Light*. I believe when we learn to be the light we will want to love on everyone. The part I sing the loudest is, "I just wanna love on everyone; all I have is yours to give." By then the dogs are howling and people are running away.

Athletes do amazing things. They train to do things that are humanly impossible. I am back in the gym, and I am learning to lift a little more each week. But I couldn't come back and do what I was doing two years ago. The same is true with running. I can't just run seven miles like I did years ago. Honestly, I run, walk, or jog. I simply run, and when I can't go any further, I walk. The same is true with loving Jesus. Spiritual training is "on purpose training" and takes discipline. Behavioral changes require time on task. I guarantee once you spend the time in His Word, loving Him with all your heart, your spirit simply develops. I don't think you could change it if you wanted to because He is irresistible. Once you love Jesus supremely, loving others becomes easier.

Craig Groeschel hit the nail on the head in his book, *Weird*, when he addressed part-time lover. "I was devastated and knew I had to refocus on my first love if I was ever going to become more like Christ and minister to others in His Name."[26] He further challenges us not to be full-time business people and part-time followers of Christ. Being part-time lovers, if you will, yields part-time spiritual results at best. We know what we get in our relationships when we are part-time lovers.

The following is taken from an old journal of mine. I hope you find it helpful.

I want to Love as a habit. I want to be like Jesus, but how?
I must be faithful habitually, reading His Word. If I want
to achieve greatness or excellence in Christ Jesus, I must

allow God to be my trainer. It is no different than the gym or anything else we want to become good at. I must work hard and refuse to take shortcuts.

I encourage you to take a notebook and start a journal. Sit with God and ask Him to reveal to you what He wants you to do regarding love or anything else for that matter. You will be surprised at how quickly the page fills, and how you can train yourself to hear God by this simple exercise. Start with this scripture, "Search me, O God, and know my heart; test me and know my anxious thoughts. See if there is any offensive way in me, and lead me in the way everlasting" (Psalm 139:23-24 NIV).

Do you ever feel a little preoccupied? Are you focused on laundry or a mental list when one of your children or even your spouse reaches out to you? I am guilty of this, but God is showing me in a loving way to stop what I'm doing and make time. Recently, I had made a call to Beth Moore. I was praying she would return the call. The phone rang and the caller I.D. said someone else's name. I started to ignore it and continue my Morning Prayer ritual when God prompted me to answer this person by showing His love, and making time for someone who needed me as much as I needed someone else.

Janice: Many distractions vie for our time. Taking the time to truly stop and listen takes a heart dedicated to others and not self. There is always going to be things to do and tasks to complete. Distractions are a way Satan takes us from an intimate relationship with God. If we don't spend time with our spouses or our children, our relationships suffer and communication is disrupted. This is also true of our relationship with God. We need to keep ourselves open to Him at all times by reading His Word, praying, and listening for His guidance.

Deb: Do you accept your Heavenly Father's love? Or do you let the demands of the day get in front of His love for you? We can busy ourselves to the point of not hearing Him. God delights in us, but do we enjoy our time with Him? I ask you to ponder what a good relationship looks like. I know one of my favorite pictures is: "The LORD thy God in the midst of thee [is] mighty; he will save, he will rejoice over thee with joy; he will rest in his love, he will joy over thee with singing" (Zephaniah 3:17). Just knowing He sings over us gives me great comfort. I personally want to know God in an exceptional way, not just an ordinary or casual way. I don't want to miss out on His love. I want to experience all God has for me.

I had an old friend who used to ask, "Do you know who you are and whose you are?"

Today my reply is, "I am a precious child of the King, opening myself to His amazing love, and hopefully pouring that love out on others."

I am ashamed to say I'm guilty of stopping love dead in its tracks. If I am overly tired, I fail to cherish a helping hand from my husband or take notice of a good deed from one of my children; not to mention taking the time to just feel the love of Jesus. Folks we have to remain present and thankful to feel God and the many ways we are loved. There are times I follow my own teachings. I start each day with a list and upon rising, I write down five things I'm thankful for. Then I begin to praise God for all He has done and is doing. I am then prepared to start my day as a thankful servant verses a demanding troubled child. In writing down what we are thankful for, we might ponder family, food, friends, our homes, cars, and stuff. But then we must dwell on our own personal relationship with our Lord and Savior Jesus Christ, and all the sunrises, sunsets, our closeness to Him, the things He has delivered us from, or brought us to. Then our blessings and our praise of thanksgiving becomes innumerable.

Janice: King David understood thanksgiving when he wrote, "Enter into his gates with thanksgiving, [and] into his courts with praise: be thankful unto him, [and] bless his name" (Psalm 100:4). Thanksgiving is not only thanking God for the good things in our lives, but it is also confessing the name of God. Confessing God's name is our declaration that only He can meet our needs because He has all the answers. In my prayer closet I focus on being thankful and becoming more like Christ. I pray the Word of God because it is powerful, and God is moved by His Word. "So shall my word be that goeth forth out of my mouth: it shall not return unto me void, but it shall accomplish that which I please, and it shall prosper [in the thing] whereto I sent it" (Isaiah 55:11).

Deb: When you open your heart and become thankful, you allow room for Him to come in and heal your brokenness. It's actually speaking a love language to our Heavenly Father.

Chapter 11

There is Hope

Now the God of hope fill you with all joy and peace in believing, that ye may abound in hope, through the power of the Holy Ghost. (Romans 5:13)

Hope

By Janice Davis

Hope gives rise to hidden dreams

Nurturing moments of sweet expectation

Securely resting as each day dawns

Offering no thought or hesitation

Hope rests intimately in our bosoms

Centered upon our trusting hearts

Our gaze slumbers quietly on the horizon

Oh! The wondrous grace it imparts

Hope is forever supernal

Springing from a grateful heart

Our veiled desires come full circle
Never, never to depart

Janice: Twenty-eight years ago my life was very different than it is today. Those who knew me considered me odd. I was someone most people wanted to stay away from. I was rejected not only by those who knew me, but also by the church I attended. As I realized many years later, they didn't want my emotional problems to tarnish their well-groomed image. Churches should be a hospital for the emotionally bruised and spiritually broken, but unfortunately too many churches are looking for folks who are emotionally well without the hindrance of personal problems. I can see now that all I ever wanted was a warm touch and human understanding. I know I came across as needy. I was indeed an emotional basket case. A jumbled mess with enormous emotional problems would have described me well.

I was fully aware I was different from most people, and can see now why people were afraid to reach out to me; I simply wasn't what you would call normal. When a small problem came up it always seemed larger than it actually was. I couldn't handle problems without my life spinning out of control. I questioned myself and God regularly, wondering why and how I got this way. This was only the beginning to me becoming emotionally whole. Looking back now I'm amazed I even survived! Inside I was screaming at the top of my lungs for help, and in my desperation I cried out to God. I didn't know what I was asking for. If I had known what it would take to bring about emotional healing, I probably would have changed my mind. But God in His divine grace and mercy didn't allow me to see that far ahead.

Deb: Janice, we often laugh and say how weird we are. To quote Craig Groeschel, author of *Weird*, "We are weird in a God way."[27]

Janice: Deb, I do agree we are honestly "weird" in a God way. How else would He have chosen two complete strangers to write a book together?

But ye [are] a chosen generation, a royal priesthood, an holy nation, a peculiar people; that ye should shew forth the praises of him who hath called you out of darkness into his marvelous light. (1 Peter 4:9)

Deb: Well, Janice, you are right about today's church. We as Christians need to learn to love like Jesus. I say learn because we aren't naturally born to love, forgive or have hope. We learn from reading the Word.

Janice: You are right again! We learn from each other and from the Word of God. His Word offers hope by teaching us to have faith in Him. Then it is played out in our lives as we give ourselves over to His truth.

Deb: Faith is not faith until we've acted upon it or exercised it. I look back at the dilemmas in my life and know that my faith and hope were weak and unexercised. Through the tragedies in my life, I have exercised faith enough that hope is automatic—hope is unseen. How often do we hear, "I hope and pray?" Hope is all things.

Merriam-Webster dictionary defines "hope" as, "to expect with confidence."[28] When we are little children we are constantly warned not to get our hopes up too high. That is the single most negative thing I recall as a child. I was constantly putting forth effort to keep from being hurt. Hope is of faith—as negative is from positive. I teach my children that God is their hope and encourage them to pray about all situations. I tell them God's answers don't always look like what you might expect, but in every instance His ways make my hopes and desires look lame. His best is better than my best, and at the end of the day it may be far better than we can imagine. "He is in the details,"[29] to quote the author of the *The Shack*, William P. Young. If we believe He is the Alpha and Omega, the Beginning and End, then we certainly know He knows what He's doing and what is good for us. I wish there was a short cut to all of this, but I think **life** and its lessons begin to show us that there is always **hope**, and that is one thing people can't take from us!

And now abideth faith, hope, charity, these three; but the greatest of these [is] charity. (1 Corinthians 13:13)

"My hope is built on nothing less than Jesus' blood and righteousness, I dare not trust the sweetest frame, but wholly lean on Jesus' Name. On Christ the solid rock I stand, all other ground is sinking sand" (Edward Mote). WOW! Do you think He is the same yesterday, today, and forever more? Don't you believe that God, who allowed every word in the Bible to be written to all those groups— the Corinthians, the Jews, and to us—smiled knowing that we would also read those exact words, and they are still applicable to us today? The same holds true with this song. The words were written by Edward Mote in 1834. I imagine he had been there, done that, and yes, got the t-shirt. He had walked in Christian faith and had a heart for Him. Let's pause and "Google him" for a moment. My kids and I have a joke when anyone asks a halfway interesting question. We first refer to the Bible and then we say, "Google it, let's see what they have to say," then someone always asks, "Who are 'they'?" We laugh as though it was the first time anyone had asked that question.

One morning it came into my mind as I went to labor, to write a hymn on the 'Gracious Experience of a Christian.' As I went up Holborn I had the chorus, On Christ the solid rock I stand, all other ground is sinking sand. In the day I had four first verses complete, and wrote them off. On the Sabbath following I met brother King as I came out of Lisle Street Meeting…who informed me that his wife was very ill, and asked me to call and see her. I had an early tea, and called afterwards. He said that it was his usual custom to sing a hymn, read a portion, and engage in prayer, before he went to meeting. He looked for his hymn-book but could find it nowhere. I said, 'I have some verses in my pocket; if he liked, we would sing them.' We did, and his wife enjoyed them so much, that after service he asked me, as a favor, to leave a copy of them for his wife. I went home, and by the fireside composed the last two verses, wrote the whole

off, and took them to sister King...As these verses so met

the dying woman's case, my attention to them was the more

arrested, and I had a thousand printed for distribution. I sent

one to the Spiritual Magazine, without my initials, which

appeared some time after this. Brother Rees, of Crown Street,

Soho, brought out an edition of hymns [1836], and this hymn

was in it. David Denham introduced it [1837] with Rees'

name and others after...Your inserting this brief outline may

in future shield me from the charge of stealth, and be a vindi-

cation of truthfulness in my connection with the Church of

God.[30] *(Edward Mote, Letter to the Gospel Herald)*

So, because God tells me this so often, I leave you with the song
in its entirety:

My hope is built on nothing less
Than Jesus' blood and righteousness.
I dare not trust the sweetest frame
but wholly trust in Jesus' Name.
Refrain
On Christ the solid Rock I stand
all other ground is sinking sand
all other ground is sinking sand.
When darkness seems to hide His face

I rest on His unchanging grace.

In every high and stormy gale

my anchor holds within the veil.

Refrain

His oath, His covenant, His blood

Support me in the whelming flood.

When all around my soul gives way

He then is all my Hope and Stay.

Refrain

When He shall come with trumpet sound

Oh may I then in Him be found.

Dressed in His righteousness alone

Faultless to stand before the throne.

Aren't the lyrics of that song more than impressive? I believe it leaves us with great hope. The song reminds me of a scripture in Corinthians. "For other foundation can no man lay than that is laid, which is Jesus Christ" (1 Corinthians 3:11 NIV).

Janice: I remember singing this song as a child, and how it provided hope for me. Although it was written many years ago, its meaning is still the same, remaining true for all who are in search of Christ, the rock of eternal hope.

DEB: There is only One who remains the same, and that is God and His most Holy Word. As we read the scriptures, the Word falls on our ears, hearts, and souls differently. As a child we memorized scripture in Sunday school because we loved Jesus. As an adult we memorize scripture not only because we love Him, but because we want to grow up spiritually, and mature so that we become more like Him. As we grow in His love and forgiveness, bravely facing our "stuff," words and knowledge take on new meaning. Last week in The Hilton Head paper, the Heraclitus quote was plastered on the front page. "No man ever steps in the same river twice, for it's not the same river and he's not the same man."[31] As I read it, I fell in love with it. I exclaimed to my husband how true the quote is concerning our lives. Imagine stepping into the same river five minutes later, the pebbles, sand, and water have all shifted substantially just as we have, even five minutes later, in that our thoughts are in another place. Imagine that same river years later, how we have grown more wise through Christ Jesus our Lord. Oh, how the lessons of life come into play. We are ever changing, literally moment to moment. This **moves** me!

Janice: God has a way of using life's circumstances to bring about changes in our character. Changes can help to make us better parents, better spouses, better friends, and better colleagues. Tomorrow will not be the same as today, yet Christ will never change. His offer of eternal hope guarantees us a better tomorrow.

Deb: So change is something we can all be assured of and ensured of. We all need "tweaking," adjusting, if you will, for we are on a quest for something. I happen to believe it is what God has called us to. We are like a river rock being tossed about by the water, rubbing up against the sand, and allowing the rough edges to be smoothed. As we're tossed about by life's trials and storms, we become the man or woman He intends for us to be. I believe that if we could relay a message of hope to our young people it would be this: "It will be okay. You will find the path He intends for you by committing to a life of prayer and Bible reading. You will see it will get easier for you." It is really not any more complicated than this. It is **simple**, but how many young people could we convince? Talk about a scientific hypothesis. Wouldn't you love to track and compare the young people in groups of those who read, pray, and are seeking His will, with those who go off with their own agenda? Isn't this truly how life is?

Today I taught a group of ninth graders. We discussed, "God stays the same." I made the example with my fist that He is right here, and it is us who dance or orbit all around Him. I explained that as our problems increase or become larger, we move closer to God. Some things that move us closer to Him might be cancer, divorce, and major problems of all kinds. I then asked the Bible class about their secrets and insecurities, explaining that smaller problems and secrets tend to keep us away from God.

Many times it is our actual state of self-confidence that shows where we live with God. For example, if I believe in me totally I might close Him out. On the other hand, more distance will naturally occur with the, "I've got this" mentality. When the day a major crisis occurs, we find ourselves running to Him.

I get hundreds of emails a day and many phone calls from people who have "hit a wall" and need and want help **now**! They not only have started running towards God, they've made the call to the prayer warrior, "Jesus Freak," child of the King to pray with them.

Action—once we move towards Him and are asking people to pray, the walls come tumbling down and **hope** is there.

As we orbit God

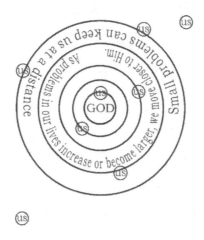

Janice: Our hope grows as we allow Him to refine us.

Deb: I believe the twelve step program of every addiction program across the United States should be implemented in our public school system. It would bring fifth graders to a new place of "finding themselves" before they end up an addict of any kind. We are all addicted to something, but it's our children we are losing at monumental rates. Twelve step programs have been found to be beneficial with all types of addictions. There are many types of "a holics" in this world. There are alcoholics, crack-a- holics, sex-a-holics, clothes-a-holics, car-a-holics, sport-a-holics, pride-a-holics, ego-a-holics, workaholics, and so on.

I personally have an addiction issue with Coke-a-Cola. Anyone who remotely knows me knows I've wrestled with it for years. I realize it is unhealthy and I still fight it. As a matter a fact, last night at my son's twenty-first birthday dinner in Charleston, SC, I had to order a coke with my dinner. The waiter was in anguish as he waited for me to render my drink order. I know he anticipated some unreal concoction of a drink so sophisticated that it was possible he wouldn't have the ingredients to make it.

As I wrestled back and forth of whether I should or shouldn't, the final moment finally came when I said with passion and surety in my voice, "I'll have a coke, not diet please, the real thing!"

WOW! The poor guy thought all of this for the rendering of a coke. If only he knew how I suffered with my Coke-a-Cola addiction. Stepping off the wagon for an evening could have started a chain reaction of cravings and did some three months later. As I proof this part of the book, I have once again vowed to give up "Coke-a-Cola," and once again I am successful with His help.

What Is It all About?

Deb: I would be willing to say that we all need more of God. We hear of people making their peace with God, people finding God, and folks who are still searching for God. Simply stated, we all need God. We need to be on the path He has chosen for each of our lives. Until then, we are busy making our peace with God.

Janice: Deb, I have often asked myself, "Can I believe God for the impossible? Am I willing to trust Him to restore me?" Many years ago I would have answered, "No." Today I can say with a sure confidence, "All things are possible for them who believe" (Mark 9:23). To those who doubt, I urge you to grab hold of those things you believe to be impossible and embrace the possibility of what can be. Although inner healing may seem elusive, hope and faith press us forward, challenging us to believe God for the impossible. We must not allow fear or fear of the unknown to stand between us and our healing. For us to claim victory over our flesh, we must come face to face with our fears. What better time than **now**?

Naturally doubts arise when we're faced with huge obstacles. I had doubts and lots of them. Embracing someone like me would require a lot of love and understanding. I just didn't know anyone willing to do that. Even friends struggled to understand me. Others ran for the hills when they saw me coming. Although I only wanted love and acceptance, people were turned off by my constant need for attention and approval. Neediness is stifling and will turn even the most loving, compassionate person away. Beloved, this isn't God's way. Man is limited in his wisdom and incapable of restoring a broken life. Others may love and encourage us, but God is the only one with the power to restore us. Run to Jesus with your problems and hang ups. Embrace Him and accept His help today.

Deb: Janice, can you tell me more about the process of restoration you are speaking of?

The Process of Restoration

Janice: I sure can. You see Deb, God never intended for any of us to be crushed by life's circumstances. The weight of sin has left us wounded and bruised in its wake. God's original intent is a life full of faith, hope, joy, and confidence in Him. Healing and restoration doesn't happen automatically when we are saved, but they are part of a journey in which God gently and lovingly deals with the unregenerate areas of our lives, one at a time. There are no quick fixes, and some answers are slower in being revealed than others. Today we live in a "Microwave Generation." We're impatient and want all our problems solved instantly. We didn't get to this place of hurt and pain overnight, and we certainly won't be healed overnight. Change will require us to look at ourselves, and confront the root cause of our problems, which is sin. The act of restoring something to its former, normal state requires an open and honest evaluation of us. If God had dealt with my sin and pain all at once, I would have been left empty, allowing Satan a door of entrance back into my life. The Holy Spirit is gentle and will not put on us more than we are able to bear.

Deb: You are preaching it now! We are a society who wants immediate gratification.

Janice: I love watching the show, *Overhaulin'*. The concept of the show is to take old cars, mostly antiques, and bring them back to their original design. The show uses a group of mechanics called the *A-Team* who have one week to remake a car. Although this particular vehicle is restored within one week, most people take their time, and some even take years to restore a vehicle to its original state.

The first step in the process is a rendering or a drawing of what the car will look like when it is restored. The next step is to completely disassemble the vehicle from the inside out. Then the real work begins. Each part is sandblasted and primed to prevent rusting, some parts are entirely replaced, then each part is individually sanded, and painted to perfection. The interior is taken apart as well, replacing every piece down to the minor details. When the last shiny coat of wet paint is applied, we have an exact replica of the original design. *Overhaulin'* is a metaphor for how God can restore us and bring us back to His original design of perfect wholeness.

Deb: Janice, I believe it! This year has been a process of restoration for me.

Janice: God wants us to look like the rendering, which is the first step in remaking us. Jesus Christ is the rendering, if you will, of what we should look like when the redemptive work of the cross is accomplished in our lives. Our goal should be to look and behave like Christ. Secondly, God must disassemble our destructive ways of thinking. In order to become like the original, we set aside old ways of thinking and behaving.

And be not conformed to this world, but be transformed by the renewing of your mind, that you may prove what is good and acceptable, and the perfect will of God. (Romans 12:2)

Transforming our thoughts will be the result of dying to ourselves, though we may suffer hardships in the process. This is a necessary step God uses to remove or sandblast away harmful habits and attitudes down to the smallest detail. Just one fisheye in the coat of a freshly painted car changes its appearance, causing the flaw to stick out like a sore thumb. Everything else about the paint itself may be perfect, but the one blemish detracts from its perfection. The same holds true for believers. Just one unregenerate flaw can hinder God's perfecting work, defeating us and delaying the finished outcome. Removing the destructive forces in our lives allows the beauty of God's perfection to shine through, bringing forth an abundance of joy and peace.

Deb: Becoming who we are in Christ takes time and attention to the details in His Word. If we were going to become a world class golfer or tennis player we would eat, sleep, and drink the sport. The same is true if we want to improve our time running marathons. To increase our skill level we would devote time to the task. I am concerned that we do not spend enough time with Him to become more of what He intends for us to become. The past six months of my life I have followed a daily regimen that has truly paid off. Every day I do the necessary daily life things such as fix breakfast, walk dogs, pack lunches, and drop the children off. Then it is time for devotions, prayer, Bible study, and work-outs on a mat in my home with Christian worship music. I sit before Christ, opening my heart to be examined by the Holy Spirit, offering prayers of thanksgiving and praise.

When I walk the dogs, I pray and sing for an hour to praise music, enjoying the presence of God. Yes, people all around Hilton Head are talking. That, coupled with fasting and praying, has allowed me to draw closer to God than I ever dreamed possible. It has also become a time of receiving instead of giving. I lead prayer groups and audiences to Him, as well as attend spiritual counseling. I will admit the last six months is the first time I haven't worked, but I didn't tell you the entire truth. I have spent my entire day in prayer and study, with the exception of taking the kids to school and walking the dogs. Therein lays the difference.

For as long as I can remember I have religiously studied my Bible and read my daily devotions, checking each off as a task to be accomplished by the end of the day. I have left everyone around me miserable, making sure I attain this daily goal. I may have snapped someone's head off if they interrupted my concentration, but, hey, it was all in God's honor, or was it? There is a huge difference when you allow Him to lead and you follow. I feel like I have been in Bible rehab and the benefits are immeasurable.

Janice: I agree with you, Deb.

Deb: For a long time I have been working on becoming more faithful to my husband. That sounded horrible! But yes, I mean more faithful in allowing Him to lead, and less of me being in control. God has focused my attention on this for quite some time. Duh? By the way, Don is praising God; he only wishes I weren't such a **slow** learner. All of us want control in some way or another. If we are married to a person who likes control it is harder to lay our control down. It is almost like two small children having to pinch the other one last. It nearly kills them if the other one gets the last pinch or hit. The same is true with we adults, we want the last say in everything. Giving into that takes the miracle of God in our lives and years of praying over it.

Christ Is the Answer

Janice: The answer to our problems lies in a relationship rooted and grounded in Christ. Through Christ all things are possible if we just believe. Believing when we can't see is what faith is all about. Many years ago I prayed and asked God to heal me. My faith was working then, though it was ever so small. Scripture tells us, "If we have faith as the grain of a mustard seed, we can say unto this mountain, be removed and cast into the sea, not doubting; nothing shall be impossible unto us" (Matthew 17:20).

Jesus used this parable to draw a clear distinction between the size of our faith and answers to prayer. Have you ever looked at the smallness of the mustard seed? Upon closer inspection, the first thing that's obvious is the mustard seed is extremely small. What isn't obvious to the naked eye though is how each little seed contains two or three seeds with the capability of producing more than a hundred seeds each. The return of just one of these small seeds can yield 800-1000 pounds per acre. Now judging with the natural eye, one would never guess its capability for huge success. But it gets even better. In more favorable conditions, just one seed alone can produce a harvest up to 1400 pounds per acre. Wow! That's success!

Now let's get back to the parallel between the mustard seed and faith. What would be considered a "favorable climate" for prayer? "Therefore if thou bring thy gift to the altar, and there remember that thy brother hath ought against thee; Leave there thy gift before the altar, and go thy way; first be reconciled to thy brother, and then come and offer thy gift" (Matthew 5:23-24). The most favorable climate for answered prayer is forgiveness. It is the key that unlocks the door. The Bible tells us that God has given to each of us a "measure of faith." Even a small amount of faith can produce an abundant harvest we can't even fathom. All it takes is just a little faith the size of a mustard seed to reap a bountiful harvest. Praying with a heart of forgiveness makes everything we desire and hope for possible as we continue in faith towards Christ. All you need is a little faith and the possibilities are endless. Let me encourage you to take that leap of faith now. I know you won't be disappointed.

Deb: A toddler learns to walk one step at a time, taking baby steps before mastering the art of running. I encourage you today, start taking baby steps toward your inner healing. Before you know it, you'll be running the race of life from a renewed perspective, giving life and hope to others along the way.

Janice: Deb, I believe we should offer our readers the opportunity to make a decision to accept Jesus Christ as Lord and Savior. Will you pray with us and make that commitment?

Dear Jesus,

I come before you a sinner, recognizing my need for Your grace and mercy. I ask for forgiveness of my sin and ask You to become the Lord and Master of my life. Please mold me and shape me into a vessel worthy of Your use. Restore my life that I may glorify You and be all You designed me to be. In Jesus' name, Amen!

Endnotes

[1]Copeland, Deb. *Attitude Therapy*. 2006 ed.

[2] Merriam-Webster. *An Encyclopedia Britannica Company*. 2006 ed.
http://www.merriam-webster.com/dictionary/identity

[3]EWTN News, Global Catholic Network. April 11, 2010.
http://www.ewtnnews.com/catholic-news/US.php?id=358#ixzz1u
VWRJKHv

[4]Lost Arts of the Mind Archive, *Can Your Heart Think and Feel?*
November 28, 2006. www.lostartsofthemind.com/2006/11/can-
your-heart-think-and-feel.html

[5]Merriam-Webster. *An Encyclopedia Britannica Company*. 2006 ed.
http://www.merriam-webster.com/dictionary/fear

[6]*The Dake Annotated Reference Bible*. 1999 ed.

[7]*The Dake Annotated Reference Bible*. 1999 ed.

[8]*The Dake Annotated Reference Bible*. 1999 ed.

[9] Meyer, Joyce. *Battlefield of the Mind*. 2000 ed.

[10]Merriam-Webster. *An Encyclopedia Britannica Company*. 2006 ed.
http://www.merriam-webster.com/dictionary/lie

[11]Wikipedia, Suicide. http://en.wikipedia.org/wiki/Suicide

[12] Hammond, Frank and Ida Mae. *Pigs in the Parlor*. 1990 ed.

[13]Merriam-Webster, *An Encyclopedia Britannica Company*. 2006 ed.
http://www.merriam-webster.com/dictionary/abandonment

[14]Strong, James. *The New Strong's Exhaustive Concordance of the Bible*. 1990 ed.

[15]Ferrell, Dr. Ana Mendez. *Iniquity*. 2011 ed.

[16]Dr. Ana Mendez. *Iniquity*. 2011 ed.

[17]Groeschel, Craig. *Weird: Because Normal Isn't Working*. 2011 ed.

[18]Swanson, Jim. *Evidence of Design*. June 12, 2009 http://www.evidenceofdesign.com/page/6/

[19]Batalion, Nathan. *Healing Talks*. 2012. http://www.healingtalks.com/health/half-of-americans-take-pharmaceutical-drugs-daily/

[20]Sawyer, Diane. *ABC News*. October 19, 2011. http://www.abcnews.go.com/Health/Wellness/10-americans-antidepressants-therapists/story

[21]Young, William P. *The Shack*. 2007 ed.

[22]Gongwer, Todd. *Lead For God's Sake*. 2011 ed.

[23]Deffinbaugh, Bob. *The Grace of God*, Part 1.http://www.bible.org/seriespage/grace-god-part-i-ephesians-15-12-21-10

[24]Wikipedia, *Binn*. http://en.wikipedia.org/wiki/Binn

[25]Vine, *W.E. Vine's Expository Dictionary of the New Testament Words*. 1996 ed.

[26] Groeschel, Craig. *Weird: Because Normal Isn't Working*. 2011 ed.

[27] Groeschel, Craig. *Weird: Because Normal Isn't Working*. 2011 ed.

[28] Merriam-Webster. *An Encyclopedia Britannica Company*. 2006 ed. http://www.merriam-webster.com/dictionary/hope

[29] Young, William p. *The Shack*. 2007 ed.

[30] Mote, Edward. *Letter to the Gospel Herald*. http://www.cyberhymnal. org/htm/m/y/myhopeis.htm

[31] Heraclitus. Wikiquote. http://en.wikiquote.org/wiki/Heraclitus

*D*eb Copeland "retired" from Corporate America to work full time for God. Copeland divides her time between Hilton Head, S.C. and Charleston, W.V. Having set aside several successful careers to answer the call of missions, she believes at the end of the day, leading people to Christ is truly all that matters. Writing this book was a direct order from God. Having said no to her future co-author for 4 months, Deb surrendered at the feet of Jesus her fears. Surrounded by a large loving family who has taught her much, she devotes the rest of her life to the passion of the nonprofit she founded; Live to Give …a GOD thing, presenting Christ to children both at home and abroad. Having survived a childhood that most couldn't, she has gone on to not only LIVE but literally, *Lives to Give*.

Janice was born and raised in southeast Georgia. She grew up in a children's home and lived there from the age of six until she graduated from high school. Later she graduated from Georgia Southern University with an Associate's Degree. Her chief desire is to offer encouragement and hope to others through her writing, using her own life experiences about emotional healing and health. She lives in Hilton Head, South Carolina, with her husband of twenty years and their three sons.

WORKS CITED

ABC News. http://abcnews.go.com/Health/Wellness/10-americans-antidepressants-therapist/storyABC News with Diane Sawyer; Courtney Hutchison, ABC News Medical Unit; October 19, 2011.

Alternative Field Crops Manual. Department of Agronomy, College of Agricultural and Life Sciences and Cooperative Extension Service, University of Wisconsin-Madison, WI http://www.hort.purdue.edu/newcrop/afcm/mustard.html.

Batalion, Nathan. http://www.healingtalks.com/health/half-of-americans-take-pharmaceutical-drugs-daily/© 2012 Healing Talks Powered by Wordpress, Nathan Batalion, Global Health Activist, Healingtalks Editor.

Dake, Finis Jennings. *Dake's Annotated Reference Bible.* Lawrenceville, GA, standard ed. 1991.

Deffinbaugh, Bob. The Grace of God, Part 1 http://bible.org/seriespage/grace-god-part-i-ephesians-15-12-21-10.

Ferrell, Dr. Ana Mendez. *Iniquity* (Ana Mendez Ferrell, Inc.)2011 www.voiceofthelight.com.

Gongwer, Todd. *Lead for God's Sake*. Copyright @ 2010 by Todd Gongwer

Published by Tyndale House Publishers, Inc. in 2011, Carol Stream, Illinois.

Groeschel, Craig. *Weird Because Normal isn't Working*. Copyright @ 2011 by Craig Groeschel Published by Zondervan Grand Rapids, Michigan 49530.

Hammond, Frank and Ida Mae. *Pigs in the Parlor,*

http://chosenexplosion.com/TrainingCenter/PathwaysFreedom/MicrosoftWordAppendixDemonGroupings.pdf.

Lost Arts of the Mind Newsletters. *Can Your Heart Think and Feel?* Nov 28, 2006 www.lostartsofthemind.com/2006/11/can-your-heart-think-and-feel.html.

Merriam-Webster, *An Encyclopedia Britannica Company*. 2006 ed. http://www.merriam-webster.com/dictionary/abandonment.

Meyer, Joyce. *Battlefield of the Mind*. Copyright @ 2000 by Joyce Meyer

Life in the Word, Inc., Publisher Warner Books, Inc., 1271 Ave of the Americas. New York, NY 10020.

Record percentage of U.S. children born out of wedlock, April 11, 2012. http://www.ewtnnews.com/catholic-news/US.php?id=358#ixzz1uVWRJKHv.

Strong, James. *The New Strong's Exhaustive Concordance of the Bible* Nashville, TN. 1990.

Swanson, Jim. *Palm Trees, Creation Evidence*

http://www.evidenceofdesign.com/page/6/, 12 June 2009.

Vine, W. E. *Love* (Noun and Verb). *Vine's Expository Dictionary of New Testament Words,* Blue Letter Bible, 1940 24 June, 1996 17 Mar 2012.

Wikipedia. *Quarry*. http://en.wikipedia.org/wiki/Lengenbach; Quarry; 30 December 2011

Wikipedia® is a registered trademark of the Wikimedia Foundation, Inc.

Wikipedia, *Social Behavior*. http://en.wikipedia.org/wiki/Elephants.

Wikipedia. *Suicide*. http://en.wikipedia.org/wiki/Suicide.

Young, William Paul. *The Shack*. Copyright @ 2007 by William P. Young

Published by Windblown Media, 4680 Calle Norte, Newbury Park, CA.

Flatts, Rascal. "Why." Unstoppable Lyric Street Records, 2009.

Sligh,Chris. "Empty Me" (Single). Brash Records, 2008.

Tomlin, Chris. "You Are My King" (Amazing Love Album).

Sparrow Records, 2000.

Beatles. "Yesterday" (Yesterday and Today Album) Capitol Records, 1966.

McKnight, Jimmy The Potters House

Flint, Anne J. "He Giveth More Grace" Public Domain

Johnston, Julia H., "Grace Greater Than Our Sin" Public Domain

Mote, Edward, "The Solid Rock" Public Domain

CPSIA information can be obtained at www.ICGtesting.com
Printed in the USA
LVOW041238080912

297914LV00002B/1/P